D0482191

# GENE KEADY

## The Truth and
## Nothing but the Truth

**Gene Keady**
*with*
**Jeff Washburn**

*Foreword by*
**Bruce Weber**

**www.SportsPublishingLLC.com**

ISBN: 1-59670-108-0

© 2005 by Gene Keady and Jeff Washburn

All rights reserved. Except for use in a review, the reproduction or utilization of this work in any form or by any electronic, mechanical, or other means, now known or hereafter invented, including xerography, photocopying, and recording, and in any information storage and retrieval system, is forbidden without the written permission of the publisher.

Publishers: Peter L. Bannon and Joseph J. Bannon Sr.
Senior managing editor: Susan M. Moyer
Acquisitions editor: Mike Pearson
Developmental editor: Doug Hoepker
Art director: K. Jeffrey Higgerson
Dust jacket design: Dustin Hubbart
Interior layout: Joseph Brumleve and Jim Henehan
Imaging: Kenneth J. O'Brien
Photo editor: Erin Linden-Levy
Media and promotions managers: Nick Obradovich (regional),
     Randy Fouts (national), Maurey Williamson (print)

Printed in the United States of America

Sports Publishing L.L.C.
804 North Neil Street
Champaign, IL 61820

Phone: 1-877-424-2665
Fax: 217-363-2073
www.SportsPublishingLLC.com

*This book is dedicated to my loving wife, Pat, who always has been there for me as a person for whom I have the deepest respect, and to our beloved daughter, Lisa, who passed away in June, 2005.*

*I also want to thank my father, Lloyd, for the values and honesty he taught me, and my mother, Mary Helen, who emphasized the importance of family and education from the time I was a young boy.*

*—Gene Keady*

CONCORDIA UNIVERSITY LIBRARY
PORTLAND. OR 97211

# CONTENTS

# ACKNOWLEDGMENTS

I want to thank all of my coaches—from youth league baseball through high school, junior college, and Kansas State University. I want to acknowledge my former players at Beloit High School in Kansas, where they learned the game of basketball from a man who was learning to coach. Thanks also go to Sam Butterfield, who helped me move into college coaching at Hutchinson (Kansas) Junior College, and Eddie Sutton, the current Oklahoma State coach who hired me as an assistant at Arkansas in the mid-1970s.

I must acknowledge the good people at Western Kentucky for having confidence in my ability to be a Division I head coach, and I must thank former Purdue athletic director George King for bringing me to West Lafayette in April, 1980, beginning a wonderful 25-year career with the Boilermakers.

My Purdue experience was enhanced by many, including former Boilermaker coaches and administrators Bob DeMoss, Dale Samuels, Fred Schaus, Bob King, Dave Alexander, Dr. John Hicks, and Morgan Burke. I want to thank our medical staff at Purdue, including athletic trainers Larry Leverenz and Denny Miller, strength and conditioning coach Greg Lehman, facilities manager Butch Brose, and my loyal secretary Kathy O'Brien, who assisted me for my final 14 seasons at Purdue. Thanks also to our sports information department, including Tom Shupe, Mark Adams, Steve Allen, Jim Vruggink, and Elliot Bloom. And of course, I must thank all my former players and assistant coaches who helped create what is known as "The Purdue Basketball Family."

I would also like to thank the media, especially Purdue Radio Network play-by-play announcer Larry Clisby and our newspaper beat writers, for their fairness and accuracy in covering Boilermaker basketball.

Last, but certainly not least, I want to extend my appreciation to all the wonderful Purdue alumni and fans who supported our men's basketball program during my 25 wonderful years as head coach.

—*Gene Keady*

# FOREWORD

## *by Bruce Weber*
### *University of Illinois Head Basketball Coach*

**O**nly one man has had as much influence on my life as my father, and that is Gene Keady. Nearly every decision I make regarding our basketball team is based on observing Coach during our 19 years together.

Purdue won six Big Ten championships during the 18 years I was on Coach's staff in West Lafayette, including three in a row from 1994 to 1996 with three distinctly different teams. In my opinion, no one got more out of the talent on his teams and no one was better at getting players to understand their roles on the team than Coach. I watched and learned as he dealt with different personalities, different teams, and different problems. I am extremely thankful that he gave me the opportunity to join his staff, and I'm glad that he's a large part of my life.

From the moment I was offered a position as a graduate assistant at Western Kentucky until I had the fortune of going along with Coach to Purdue, and continuing through my experiences at Southern Illinois and now the University of Illinois, I have used his principles in making life decisions as well as decisions in how to handle every situation I have encountered as a coach.

After the outstanding season we had in 2005, I was fortunate enough to be recognized as national coach of the year by several different organizations. At each award ceremony I could only think of the impact that Coach Keady had on my career. It was very special to have Coach as presenter for a couple of the awards. As we made our journey to the Final Four, I often thought how I so wished Coach could have experienced a Final Four on the sideline. It would have been a fitting achievement for a great coach and a great person.

As a naïve, young basketball coach, I thought it would be easy to break into the collegiate level. I found out through a friend that Western Kentucky was looking for a graduate assistant, and after talking with Gene Keady by phone, he told me to drive down to Bowling Green and speak with him in person about the job. My brother and I drove straight through from Milwaukee only to find out that Coach was not in town for a couple of days. So we turned around and drove back to Milwaukee feeling very disappointed about the entire situation. While working a camp at home, I spoke with Coach again from a pay phone. He apologized for not being there and asked me to come back down. I simply told him I couldn't afford to take the time to drive back to Kentucky, and that if he wanted me on his staff, he would have to offer me the job over the phone. Well, I was lucky he did just that on that day, and it began a wonderful 26-year relationship.

When people watch Coach on the sidelines, all they see is an intense competitor with a fiery personality. Off the court, I saw a big puppy dog with a great sense of humor. It's quite a contrast. He took over a difficult situation at Purdue with an intense rivalry against Indiana University and Bob Knight. Despite having several opportunities to move elsewhere and with many people telling him to seek other coaching positions, Coach Keady stuck with it for 25 incredible years. In my opinion, there is no question he should be a Hall of Famer.

This book is a fitting tribute to a fantastic coach who is an even better person. He has given the best part of his life to Purdue University and the Boilermaker basketball program. I am proud to have been a small part of his life. I hope you enjoy learning more about this special person.

## CHAPTER ONE

# Growing Up in Larned

**M**y dad, Lloyd Keady, quit school after the eighth grade in order to help earn money to make it possible for his brother to attend college. Dad went to work at the only greenhouse in Larned, Kansas, for Mr. Henry Gilbert, a man who came to the United States from Germany and opened the business. The greenhouse began as a retail facility, where they specialized in weddings, funerals, and all holidays. But that challenge soon became overwhelming for the small staff. They had so much business that they frequently worked 48 hours in a row without sleep. The men worked so hard that dad caught pneumonia—and almost died from it—in 1940 when I was four years old. In response, Mr. Gilbert changed to a wholesale format to reduce the workload. He primarily sold geraniums, mums, tomato plants, and the like, to other greenhouses.

From the very beginning of my life, it was evident that education would be a priority for me. That's because Mom valued education and impressed its importance on me. When World War II began, I entered first grade and attended Third Ward Grade School. I did not attend kindergarten, because we didn't have one in Larned. I had an excellent first-grade teacher, which reminds me of the excellent, thorough teaching staffs that existed within the various Kansas school systems. I participated in an enjoyable educational experience, knowing in hindsight that I was taught correctly.

Those school-related experiences bring back fond memories. I can remember walking from Third Ward Schoolhouse past the home of the family that owned the Cobb Electric Company in Larned. They had two sons who were real ornery. At that time, those boys were in junior high school and owned a German Shepherd. I was scared to death to walk past that house, so I would run like hell past it.

Before my second-grade year, my family relocated to a farm where dad found employment. That year I attended a one-room schoolhouse for grades one through eight. I was the only second-grader among 15 students, and the schoolhouse was heated by a pot-belly stove. Since the school was located about three miles from the farm on which we were living, on my first day of second grade my dad let me ride a Shetland Pony to school. I had to cross a creek to get to the main road from the farmhouse. Shetland Ponies are bad-tempered animals, as I found out. I was wearing my new school clothes, and when we reached the middle of that creek, the pony stopped and rolled over with me still on it. So I spent my first day of

**Sporting overalls during my second-grade year. For three years, I lived on a farm where my dad was employed.** *Courtesy of Gene Keady*

second grade in wet clothes. But the experience in that one-room schoolhouse was a good one. I always liked my teachers, and I enjoyed having people around me. I wasn't a brown-noser; I just really liked going to school.

In third and fourth grade I attended classes in another school in Deighton, Kansas, which is 10 miles from where we lived. The one-room schoolhouse near the farm was vacated. Then, as World War II was about to end, we moved to a farm near Garfield, Kansas, and dad went back to work for Mr. Gilbert in Larned. During fifth grade, I got to ride to school on a bus for the first time. During that year in school, I began to enjoy reading, although I probably didn't act like it at that time. However, my attitude about reading changed when a polio epidemic broke out, and school was cancelled for a six-week period. I was quite happy about that. My uncle drove a road grater, and since we lived on a farm, the grater was stored with us. At the time, I was hoping that I would be allowed to ride the road grater with my uncle. I also wanted to do the sort of things that all kids enjoy: play in the pasture and shoot my slingshot. Using my slingshot, I often took aim at the rabbits that roamed the pasture. I never hit one of them, but I always tried. So with school out for six weeks, I anticipated doing lots of fun activities.

Boy, was I was wrong. Mom went to the Garfield library and checked out lots of books. I was instructed to read a book every day. That is how Mother kept my mind alert during the six weeks that school was not in session. She wanted to keep me sharp academically and keep me interested in reading. When the polio epidemic ended, we attended school on Saturdays to make up for the lost time. I realized then that the break really wasn't such a fun thing after all.

In sixth grade, I learned that Kansas was home to fighter pilot training bases in Dodge City, Garden City, Pratt, and Great Bend. In those towns, the United States government built landing strips, and each one had barracks. Dad bought one of those Air Force barracks in Pratt and moved it to 512 East Third Street in Larned. That's where I resided from the time I entered sixth grade on through high school. I was back in school in Larned, and I was happy. My childhood was fun, despite the fact that we didn't have any money—which I didn't know at the time. I knew only that we always had food on the table. We didn't live in a nice home, but my sister and I were happy. She probably would dispute that, because she was fed up with the sporting world. Everything in our home was geared towards sports, which I loved. So my sister—as she often reminds me—was left out of a lot of things.

But my family was great. Dad was the most solid man I've ever known. He was a person of integrity, an honest man. I never heard him tell a lie to anyone. As someone who worked in the greenhouse business, he got to meet a variety of people, and he was well-liked. I never heard anyone say anything bad about my dad. Before he married Mom, Dad also worked in a pool hall after his day at the greenhouse ended. He made extra money and became the pool hall's shark. He would play guys who came into the pool hall for money—even for the house. I wish I could play pool as well as my father played. He also had an unusual hobby. From what I understand, he liked to box and was a boxer as a young man.

My mother worked as a cook at the hospital when she met my father. My dad was a strong figure within our home, but my mother provided balance with her emphasis on education, family, and home. Together they provided an excellent upbringing for my sister and me. Everyone knew I loved sports, but everyone also knew that if Gene Keady was going to participate in athletics, other priorities would have to be met before I had a ball in my hands.

✦ ✦ ✦ ✦

While I had always enjoyed athletics, sports first began to be a big part of my life during sixth-grade recess, during which we played softball. My junior high school coach, Merwin Wilson, encouraged all the boys in my class to go out for track and field. He would load us into school buses when we were seventh-graders and take us to high school track and field meets. He wanted us to observe high school kids competing. "See, if you finish first, second, or third," he would say, "then they will give you a medal." That was our motivation, and he nurtured that goal.

The athletic programs in all Kansas high schools were important to the community. High school coaches seized every opportunity to take their players to Kansas State, Kansas, Wichita State, or Fort Hays State for a football game. In those days, it was all about collegiate games, as we didn't have opportunities to attend professional sporting events. The closest professional team to us was the Kansas City Blues, which was a New York Yankees minor league team. That is how I became a Yankee fan.

When I was in third grade, Dad took me to Scott City, Kansas, to play in a basketball tournament for third-graders. We never practiced; we just went to the event and played. Now, I can't believe that we did that. No practice! That was my first basketball game, and all I really remember about it was that our uniforms were green and white. The next time I played organized basketball was in junior high school in Larned, where our colors were black and orange. As eighth-graders, we often played Zook, a tiny town just outside of Larned with a school of just 60 kids. By comparison, Larned was a town of 4,000 people, which was really big.

Zook beat us, but I was high-point man with eight points. I didn't know anything about how to play basketball. The recreation center in Larned allowed kids to work out there during the winter, and that's how I was introduced to the sport. The center sponsored us for an hour, and we got to dribble and shoot layups.

After the game against Zook, my dad said, "You got beat?" He asked me how many times our center touched the basketball. I told my dad that we didn't throw the ball to the center. Dad said, "No wonder you didn't win." That was my first lesson in how to play the game correctly. My dad was not a well-educated man, but he was a wise man.

It turned out that those kids from Zook who beat us became really good friends of mine. Those same kids won the state tournament when they were seniors in high school at their class level, which was a smaller class than Larned.

Those kids from Zook weren't just good at basketball, either. The same group was undefeated in six-man football. The guy who played center for Zook's football and basketball teams—Harley Kassellman—went to Garden City Junior College with me and was our center on the football team there. I was the quarterback, and we never had a center/quarterback fumble exchange in two seasons.

At that time, there weren't many ways other than sports to entertain one's self. The only entertainment we had was a black-and-white television. We always watched Jackie Gleason and Red Skelton, too. So sports were a big deal for me. At that time, I also played summer recreation baseball and benefited from having a great coach. The coach of my team was Washburn University's baseball and basketball coach. His hometown was Larned, so he came back each summer to work. Baseball was big in a town the size of Larned. We had American Legion Baseball and a league known as the Ban Johnson League, which was comprised of a group of college players. And there also were town teams. So we always had a place to play or watch baseball in Larned.

I enjoyed baseball, and I was good at it, too. When I played American Legion ball, I made the All-State team as a third baseman. We squared off against the Missouri All-Stars. Our team was good as well. We advanced to the state tournament but did not win it.

But I was also focused on winning medals in other sports. I loved competing in track during junior high. I continued to participate through high school, and during my senior year our track team finished second in the state finals, missing the championship by half a point. Billy Mills, an American Indian who won the 10,000 meters at the 1964

**Playing catch as a 13-year-old. Baseball was big in the town of Larned, and I followed the New York Yankees because their minor league team was stationed in Kansas City.**
*Courtesy of Gene Keady*

Summer Olympic Games, led the team that beat us. He attended Haskell Institute in Lawrence, Kansas, and they beat us by half a point.

We had the state shot put champion, Jim Blackwell, and the 100-yard dash champion and my best friend, Troy Young, on our high school team. They called me the silver medal guy, because I was always placed second, scoring points in the shot put, the discus, and maybe the 220. I was kind of our track team's utility guy. But that was good for me, because I learned to run. I had developed an excellent technique in the shot put and in the discus, so when I was a senior in high school, they let me teach junior high school kids. My high school coach told me, "If you are interested in coaching, why don't you step up and show them what you have learned?"

As a high school athlete, my teams weren't very good. We didn't win many games. As much team speed as we had—as evidenced by our successful track team—we should have been better. But in basketball and football, there were a lot of good teams in our conference. Russell High School was in our league, and they won a lot of state championships. Many of their kids went to Kansas University and played basketball. Larned was probably the smallest school in our league.

My senior year in high school, we were 4-4 in football. I was our quarterback, and I was a good passer, but I probably should have run more. I tried to get the ball to the halfbacks. In basketball, we were okay. My third cousin—Harry Vincent—was my high school basketball coach, but Harry didn't play me much. Being someone's relative in those days didn't mean anything, which is the way it should be.

In Larned we played baseball in the summer, football in the fall, basketball in the winter, and ran track in the spring.

That was a typical schedule for a Kansas athlete—if you really loved sports—in the 1940s and 1950s. All my buddies did that, and we had fun together. Troy Young's father and mother were farmers who lived about eight miles outside of Larned. Troy and I spent a lot of time together. He would spend one Saturday night at my house, and I would spend the next at his. Dean Miller, Larry Douglass, Troy, and I were all buddies. Dean's father was a farmer as well, and Dean got to drive a convertible when we were juniors in high school. Boy, did we think we were hot stuff! We drove down Main Street, and "dragging" down Main Street was a big deal. The four of us just hung around together.

Along with participating in athletics, I worked alongside dad at the greenhouse. I began working there as a sixth-grader, and by the time I was in high school, they let me wait on customers. That experience taught me a work ethic. I worked from 8 a.m. until 5 p.m., and I had to be on time. To see if I really wanted to work, Mr. Gilbert would make me take old newspapers down into the basement and unfold them. We wrapped all of our flowers in paper. There was a flat drawer on the counter, and when they pulled it out, there would be paper right there to wrap the flowers. I made sure all the papers were flat. I would go downstairs and unfold newspapers for eight hours in a row. Boy, did I learn self-discipline from that task. After I got a little bit older, Mr. Gilbert had me do different tasks. I eventually advanced to watering the flowers.

But I really didn't enjoy that line of work. It's why I went to college. I was afraid I was going to have to work in the greenhouse like my dad. But it was a good job for me, because I learned to be responsible and that old adage, "the customer is always right." The experience also taught me that I better get

**This handsome devil was me during my senior year of high school.** *Courtesy of Gene Keady*

my college degree or I wasn't going to make much money. I watched my dad make a dollar an hour year after year.

In my free time during those years, my friends and I would gather at someone's house on Saturdays and Sundays to play cards. Someone usually had a basketball goal on his barn, and we would shoot baskets, too. Recreation was not a problem. I was either attending games, playing games, playing cards, or going someplace with friends.

Academically, I was a good—but not great—high school student, because I listened. But down the road, when I began work on my master's degree, I became a very good student. I've always had a knack for being able to listen to what people say and then comprehend it. If it was a difficult class, then I took notes. But I was in class every day. I can't remember missing a single day of school. I may have had the mumps in third grade and missed a day, but that was it. I always wanted to go to school, because that was my ticket to playing sports.

## CHAPTER TWO

# A College Man

Upon graduation from high school, I wanted to go to a bigger school at the junior college level. One of my heroes—basketball and football star Harold Patterson—had gone from Rozel, Kansas, to Garden City Junior College. Patterson had done well at Garden City, and hence went on to Kansas University, where he was an All-American. Patterson then played in the Canadian Football League, where he established a record for pass receiving. So I copied his route.

I played two years at Garden City. We played nine football games each season, 25 basketball games per year, and were really good in track and field, finishing third in the nation. During the summer, I stayed in Garden City and played in the

Ban Johnson League as an outfielder. Over the summer, I also worked in a dairy, because I had to have a summer job. When I was a freshman at Garden City, I went to class from 8 a.m. until noon, walked to a cattle yard and worked for two hours, and then went to practice at 3 p.m. I had to do that, because that's how I made my money for room and board. As an athlete, I was provided with a scholarship for tuition and books but not room and board.

My first semester at Garden City was an excellent experience in the classroom. I was so afraid that I might flunk out of school and have to go home to Larned that I spent lots of time on my studies and made the honor roll with a grade-point average between 3.0 and 3.9. After that first semester I didn't bear down quite as hard, but I continued to do pretty well in the classroom. While I was at Garden City, I strove to earn my degree so that I could live at a higher standard. I wanted to have a better life than my parents in terms of finances.

At Garden City, Jack Morris was my football and track coach. Jack flew a crop spray plane during the summer. That guy was a piece of work, but he was good for me. I was pretty ornery at the time. On the bus, I would get pretty loud, and sometimes he would make me sit up front with him. In football, I was our quarterback, and we won the league when I was a sophomore. We got third in the nation in track that same year, so that was a pretty good year.

To add to the excitement, during my sophomore year at Garden City we also went to the national tournament for basketball. I made 13 field goals in my final basketball game during the tournament at Hutchinson Junior College in Kansas. We got in the locker room after we were defeated, and

**I was told that I "shot too much" during my sophomore year at Garden City Junior College.** *Courtesy of Gene Keady*

the first thing head coach Don Talley said to me was, "You shot too much."

My time at Garden City proved to be worthwhile in the long term. The president at Garden City during my time there, Dr. Andy Elland, eventually took a job at Hutchinson Junior College. Due to that connection, years later I would get the basketball head coaching position at Hutchinson. In addition to Elland, the high school basketball coach at Garden City was Sam Butterfield, whose team practiced from 1 p.m. until

3 p.m., just before Garden City Junior College took the court for practice. I got to know Sam Butterfield by sitting and talking with him as our teams were changing courts. When I later went to Kansas State University, Sam Butterfield became the head basketball coach at Hutchinson Junior College. So both the university president and head basketball coach at Hutchinson Junior College were people that I had become acquainted with while I was at Garden City.

As I neared the end of my stay at Garden City, I began to ponder my options for moving on to a Division I school. A guy named Laverne Billinger, who was a Garden City High School graduate with whom I played football, went to Kansas State on a baseball scholarship as a catcher. I lived at his parents' house for a while during my stay at Garden City. They were an old German couple who took me under their wing. When I would go out on a date, Laverne's father would let me borrow his car. I wanted to play baseball and football with him at Kansas State, so that's where I decided to go next.

I also was considering Kansas, Wichita State, Colorado, and the Air Force Academy. I went to the Air Force Academy and took their test, but I didn't know anything about trigonometry, so I wasn't going to pass that test. I also learned that you can't get into the cadet flying program at Air Force if you've ever been knocked out for more than 30 minutes. They found out that I had been hit in the head by a shot put and knocked out when I was in high school. I was dropped as a potential Air Force cadet. I was upset about that, because I really wanted to be a pilot. I had a keen interest in flying, and I wouldn't have minded being in the military. During the Korean War, I was too young to serve, and during the Vietnam War, I was teaching and already had children. Had it not been for Laverne, I probably would have gone to Colorado. They had really good athletes and had recently gone to the Orange Bowl. Colorado had a great player in Boyd Dowler, who went on to become a star wide receiver for Vince Lombardi's great Green Bay Packer teams of the 1960s.

I was well prepared to play at Kansas State. My junior college football coach was hard on us. He ran the hell out of us, and it was hot in Garden City in August. I was always in good shape. When I got to Kansas State, I was prepared for two-a-day football practices. I lost 10 pounds every practice. I weighed 194, and when I got out of practice, I weighed 184. That's how much you perspire in Kansas. They didn't let us have much water in those days. It's a wonder that all of us didn't die.

Bernard "Bus" Mertes was my head football coach at Kansas State. Bus went on to be Bud Grant's assistant with the Minnesota Vikings for many years. And we had great assistant coaches at Kansas State, too. As for the team, we had a good starting 11, but we didn't have any depth. Our opponents would wear us down. Oklahoma, coached by Bud Wilkinson, was really good in those days. Colorado and Missouri also were good. Overall, playing football was a good experience for me, because I discovered that despite good coaching and plenty of effort, talent was the key to winning games. Without great players, a college team cannot win big at the higher levels of Division I athletics.

I played in the Wing-T offense as a halfback, so I could either carry the ball or be a receiver. I had to block, too—we halfbacks hated that. I made honorable mention All-Big Eight Conference during my junior year. Then I injured my knee in my fourth game of my senior year against Colorado. In that

**I was a halfback at Kansas State, and was named All-Big Eight (honorable mention) my junior year.** *Kansas State Sports Information*

game, I ran 78 yards down to the 5-yard line and then fumbled because a defender came from behind and knocked the ball out of my hands. My shoe came off on that play. For years when I would go back to Kansas State, people would say, "Oh, yes, you are the halfback who lost his shoe on the 5-yard line." So that Colorado game is not a good memory.

For the first time since I was in sixth grade, when football season was over I didn't have to go play basketball. So I went to Tex Winter, who was the basketball coach at Kansas State, and asked him, "Any chance you would let me come out for basketball?" Tex knew me, because he had seen me play at Garden City in the national tournament. But Kansas State's basketball team was loaded, and on its way to the Final Four that year. He told me that they didn't need me, but that he would talk to the track coach and help me participate in indoor track. I went out for indoor track and ran the 60-yard dash and threw the shot put. Those events were easy to prepare for. The 60-yard dash was short.

During track season, I got to know Tex better. One time I slipped while throwing the shot, and I threw it onto the basketball court while they were practicing. He chewed me out pretty good. Then I got to be friends with Tex when I went back several years later to get my master's degree from Kansas State. He had always liked me for some reason. He lectured in some of my master's classes, and that's how I learned about the fundamentals of basketball. I really didn't know a lot about basketball fundamentals until those classes. I had just played the game without giving them any thought. My strength as a basketball player was making a jump shot.

In those days, your coaches were your teachers. One coach might teach kinesiology, the baseball coach might teach the fundamentals of baseball. You always were around your coaches, so you were afraid to miss class.

During my senior year, I took the winter off to recuperate my knee. Then, I tried out for—and made—the baseball team. I had a nice senior year playing baseball, and I could have signed with the Kansas City Athletics after my senior year. But instead I jumped at an opportunity to try out with the Pittsburgh Steelers.

## CHAPTER THREE

# Learning to Coach

After my senior year at Kansas State, the Pittsburgh Steelers drafted me, and I signed a contract for $12,000, although the contract was not guaranteed. All I was guaranteed was my expenses to travel to Pittsburgh. It was a dream come true for me. I was surrounded by players who all shared the same interest: make it to the NFL. A lot of guys with whom I played college ball didn't dream of playing professionally—they just wanted to get their degree. In this modern era, imagine that.

The four quarterbacks in camp were Len Dawson, Jack Kemp, Earl Morrall, and Bobby Layne. Buddy Parker had come over to coach from the Detroit Lions, who had just won the NFL championship. I was eager to make a good impression. In my junior year at Kansas State, I finished second in pass receiving in the Big Eight Conference behind Charlie James, who went on to play outfield for a time for the St. Louis Cardinals. I was considered a pretty good pass receiver, and that's the position I tried out for with Pittsburgh. Those four quarterbacks—all in the same camp—are what I remember most about my time in camp, which lasted about four weeks before I was released. I had a lingering knee injury, and I just didn't have any speed.

Buddy Parker told me to go home, get well, and come back in 1959 to try to be a defensive back. I was okay with that decision. I didn't care what position I played. The Steelers had seen enough of me in college to know that I could play offense and defense. During that era in college football, you had to play both ways—offense and defense. NCAA football did not have a two-platoon system during the time I played at Kansas State.

Experiencing an NFL training camp was wonderful. I rarely saw Bobby Layne, because it was exhibition season, and he rarely participated in practice. The guy I really liked was Len Dawson, who played at Purdue during the 1954, '55 and '56 seasons. Dawson was a great guy, and to me, he was like a movie star. He had a great personality and always was cordial and helpful.

But all good things come to an end, and when my NFL training camp experience was over, I was a man in need of a job. I was about to take my first step into coaching and teaching.

✦ ✦ ✦ ✦

The principal at Beloit, Kansas, High School had previously been the football coach at Beloit, but he had taken a year off to attend Kansas State and earn his administrative certificate. He was in Kansas State's education building when I was a senior at Kansas State, so he got to know me. They say that it's "all about who you know," and again, here is an example in my life when someone who knew me helped me.

The Beloit High School basketball coach—Bill Cornwell—had left to take a better job in August 1958 at Shawnee Mission North High School near Kansas City. I was home in western Kansas, and when Beloit found out that I was not with the Steelers, they asked if I was interested in the job. I was, and so I applied. At that time, the Beloit job was about the only coaching position open in Kansas. But this wasn't just a coaching position; I would also be teaching general science, physical education, economics, and psychology—plus coaching golf and assisting with football and track. I got the job, and my first contract was for $4,200.

My most challenging role of that long list was actually head golf coach. The only thing I knew at that time about golf was what I learned from caddying once in Larned at a golf outing. My dad had recommended that I caddy to earn a couple dollars. Actually, I ended up raking sand at that golf outing, and they paid me $5 for a day's work. The lowlight of the experience was that I was struck in the leg by someone's drive. That was the only time I had been around golf in my life. So to learn how to coach golf I purchased some books and studied the game.

The 1958-59 school year began, and I found myself in a classroom. I had to stay ahead of the students, so that kept me hustling. I couldn't let the students think that I didn't know what I was talking about. Here I was, teaching psychology. In my first year, I used a test out of the back of the book. I didn't know a lot about teaching psychology, but I did know the subject matter because I had taken a lot of psychology classes during college. That subject actually was pretty easy for me.

Moving out of the classroom and onto the basketball court, I have lots of fond memories from my first season as a head basketball coach, despite the fact that we had a losing record. In my second year we went to the state tournament, which was a big deal in Kansas in those days.

After my first year at Beloit, I applied for several head football coaching positions around the state, but I did not get one. To this day, I've never been hired for a job that I actually applied for. In each instance, the employer came after me. I got the job at Beloit that way, and the same was true when I left Beloit to coach at Hutchinson Junior College. When I was coaching at Beloit, Sam Butterfield was the basketball coach at Hutchinson Junior College, and he would come to Beloit to visit with students on "career day." Sam would talk to our kids about attending Hutchinson. He was a great personality, so Hutchinson sent its basketball coach to Beloit as a representative. I would sit with him at those career days.

During one of our visits, Sam said, "Because I liked you at Garden City Junior College, if you will get your master's degree, I'm thinking about retiring in four years and becoming the athletic director. I would bring you in as my assistant coach for one year, and then when I moved on as athletic director, you would become the head coach at Hutchinson." Frankly, the Hutchinson position is better than a lot of Division I coaching jobs, because the National Junior College

Tournament is staged there every year. I was excited by the proposition, so during the next three summers, I spent time at Kansas State earning my master's degree.

During those summers while I was taking master's classes, I lived in the same house as Bill Guthridge, who coached for many seasons at North Carolina. Bill would find a house, and two or three of us would live in it. After classes, Bill and I played on the same softball team. After games, we spent lots of time together at the Dairy Queen. I enjoyed my time back at Kansas State. I constantly am reminded that Kansas has more people go to college—per capita—than any state in the nation. I guess there's nothing else to do there except study. (All joking aside, that's not really true. There are lots of fun things to do in Kansas.)

Teaching and coaching at Beloit was a worthwhile experience, especially when I consider that we advanced to the state finals three times in my seven seasons there as coach. A third-place finish at state was our best. In those days, there were three classes in Kansas, and we were in Class 2A, which was the middle group. I learned a lot about coaching while at Beloit, and I experimented often with my offensive and defensive schemes. In those days, I was an offensive coach—everything I preached was about running and shooting the basketball. It was always about scoring more points than the other team. If we didn't score 100 points, I was mad. I was a good shooter, and I enjoyed teaching others how to shoot. We played a pressing style of defense, and we shot the basketball. We tried to shoot 72 times a game, a number that I got from former Kansas State and NBA coach Cotton Fitzsimmons.

Later on in my coaching career—when I was coaching at Hutchinson—we went to the national tournament six times in nine years but never won it. I was really concerned about why we couldn't win national championships. I thought it must be because I did not know a lot about defense. When I became Eddie Sutton's assistant at Arkansas in the early 1970s, I finally solidified my philosophy about defense. Early on in my career, I knew the fundamentals of the fastbreak and how to teach shooting, but until I coached under Eddie, I hadn't shored up my defensive strategy.

✦ ✦ ✦ ✦

Sure enough, once I had obtained my master's degree from Kansas State, Sam Butterfield hired me as his assistant coach at Hutchinson. When I went to Hutchinson in 1965, I found myself in a biology classroom teaching 25 hours a week, which was difficult at the time. I also was an assistant football coach until October 15. I coached the defensive backs and was a scout for them.

As basketball coach, I found it relatively easy to recruit players to Hutchinson, because we hosted the Junior College National Tournament and had a big arena there. Our facilities were our biggest edge in the recruiting battle. And our fans were great. We would have at least 6,000 for every home game, and at times we drew as many as 8,000. We recruited some players with Division I skills to attend Hutchinson as a result of those perks. The best player I coached at Hutchinson was a six-foot-10 kid from New York City named Rudy Jackson who went on to Wichita State. The best athlete we had was Richard Morsden from Wyandotte High School in Kansas City. He went on to Wichita State and made the All-Missouri Valley Conference team. Two other good players I recruited were

Kenny Weins, who went on to play at Cornell, and Courtney Rogers, who later played at Kansas State.

Despite working for a solid academic school, we faced two disadvantages in recruiting at Hutchinson. First, unlike some other junior colleges, such as Vincennes University, we could not offer room and board. Our kids at Hutchinson were required to work. Second, my athletic director would allow me to have only three out-of-state scholarships. In the Kansas junior college system, schools were allowed to give as many as five out-of-state scholarships. So that restricted my recruiting effort as well, and we really never found success recruiting the greatest players. Fred Brown, who played at Iowa, went to junior college at Burlington Junior College. Bob McAdoo went to Vincennes.

I enjoyed coaching at Hutchinson, but early in the 1970s I realized that it was time for me to move on. I applied for a couple of Division I coaching positions. In fact, I almost went to Northern Arizona as an assistant coach. They said that they would possibly promote me to head coach after a couple of seasons, but I said, "No maybes." I wanted to sign a contract that said I would become the head coach.

✦ ✦ ✦ ✦

In 1974, I learned that Eddie Sutton had an assistant coach's opening on his staff at Arkansas, so I sat down and wrote him a long letter, explaining why he should hire me. Within a week, I received a call from Eddie, who said, "Come down. We want to interview you."

The opportunity to work alongside Eddie was so valuable to me. He taught me how to coach in practice, how to recruit, and how to coach in game situations, including how to manage timeouts. He had learned from the great coach Henry Iba. I learned at Arkansas that the No. 1 thing that gets coaches fired is when they allow their players to shoot too quickly, especially if you don't have talent. I also learned from Eddie that you don't want to clamp down too hard on a player's offensive game. You have to let shooters shoot.

At Arkansas, the initial shock for me was that I didn't have to worry about teaching in the classroom. I wasn't teaching a class at 7:30 a.m. after staying up until 4 a.m. It was wonderful not to have to grade papers, give tests, and calculate grades. Finally, all I was doing was coaching. They also gave me a car to recruit, which was a huge bonus. I drove a Mercury Cougar, and I thought I was in heaven.

It was easier in those days, because I could go recruit any day of the year. There were no restrictions as there are now. Usually, we got our recruiting done by July and didn't have to worry about it any more. I was always around high school coaches. During that era, there were no Amateur Athletic Union (AAU) basketball leagues, so there wasn't the burden of dealing with additional coaches. When I was at Arkansas, a "system" recruited players. Eddie Sutton would go see players sometimes, and assistant Pat Foster would go see them sometimes. I would visit with them sometimes. We all recruited our players. The head coach making the final sell was the key to recruiting. Most people think one certain guy is a good recruiter, but that is not the way it truly is.

Later on in my career while I was at Purdue, people thought that assistant coach Frank Kendrick was a great recruiter, and that Bruce Weber was not. Now that Bruce is at Illinois and has found success with a high-profile team, all of a sudden he is now considered a great recruiter. I often read in the paper that I was not a good recruiter. But we had 16 first-team All-Big Ten players while I was at Purdue, and I recruited all of them. My entire staff supported me, but I made the final pitch.

As my career at Purdue was winding down, I really became frustrated when I had to start selling the AAU coaches in addition to everyone else. When I had to sell only the high school players and their parents, that was fine. I enjoyed that. Now, a college coach has to convince the AAU coaches, too. Some of these AAU coaches want the college coach to meet some guy who thinks that he can get this kid a shoe deal. The college coach ends up being further and further removed from the high school coach and the parents. I didn't adapt too well to those changes over the years.

But recruiting for Eddie at Arkansas was a fun time. Sydney Moncrief, who went on to a great career in the NBA, was from Little Rock, Arkansas. Marvin Delph was from Conway, Arkansas, and Ron Brewer was from Fort Smith, Arkansas, which was right down the interstate from the University of Arkansas. I would take off from Fayetteville and make three stops to recruit them all. At the time we recruited them, we did not know they were going to be that good. I also recruited Steve Shaw, who was our starting center during that time, and Alan Zahn out of Albuquerque, New Mexico.

It wasn't until after we recruited that group that we noticed how special they were as a whole. Moncrief and Brewer were very talented players and warriors, especially Moncrief. He had great skills. He could run like a deer and jump through the roof. In 1978, we went to the Final Four, which was a tremendous experience. However, as a coach, I was so busy doing so many things that the time just flew by. I

I enjoyed not having the responsibility of teaching in the classroom at Arkansas. The classroom for me was on the court, where I was the pupil learning from coach Eddie Sutton. *University of Arkansas*

was recruiting and scouting and having the time of my life. But when we were beaten, I was angry and sick. We had a great year, but we didn't win the championship, so I didn't feel like I did my job.

That 1978 Final Four featured Kentucky, Duke, Notre Dame, and Arkansas, and that's about as good as it gets. Kentucky beat us, Duke beat Notre Dame, and then Kentucky beat Duke in the National Championship game. In those days, they played a third-place game, and we beat Notre Dame in overtime when Brewer hit a huge shot.

Overall, being at Arkansas was a priceless experience for me. Funny thing is, it was during my first three years there that I learned the most, but everybody always wants to talk about my fourth year, when we advanced to the Final Four. My first year there, in 1974-75, we were pretty talented. We had a winning record that year, and the next season we won the Southwest Conference championship. In 1976-77, we also won the Southwest Conference, but Wake Forest beat us in the NCAA tournament in a game staged in Norman, Oklahoma. Eddie Sutton was so upset about that loss that he did not speak to the players over the summer. He would not talk with any of them. That loss motivated our kids for the 1977-78 season. We had good kids who played hard. Jimmy Counce was a starting forward, Shaw was the starting center, and Brewer, Moncrief, and Delph together were called "The Triplets." That team had good depth, we could run, and we could play halfcourt or fullcourt. The Arkansas fans were great, and Fayetteville is a beautiful community. It has everything from mountains to rice paddies to diamond mines. Arkansas really is what I would describe as a versatile state. And we were fortunate enough to have a versatile basketball team that year.

## CHAPTER FOUR

# Earning a Shot at Division I

In 1977, I interviewed for the Idaho State head coach job and actually took it. But as I was flying back to Arkansas through Salt Lake City, I reflected on what I had done. I thought about the fact that Arkansas had Moncrief and Brewer coming back—we were going to have a heck of team in 1977-78 at Arkansas. In a split second, I decided that I was not going to leave Arkansas. I called the Idaho State athletic director from Salt Lake City and told him that I was going to turn down his offer. Then I called Eddie Sutton from Salt Lake City, and Eddie told me that I was a dummy for turning down the Idaho State position. He said that I might never get another chance to be a Division I head coach.

The season after a team makes the Final Four, its assistant coaches—and sometimes its head coaches—are always in demand by other colleges with head coach openings. That's constantly amazed me, and it's how I landed my first Division I head coaching position at Western Kentucky in 1978. The irony—I soon discovered—is that there was probably more pressure on me to win when I was at Hutchinson Junior College than there was at Western Kentucky. The same is true for a lot of other Division I schools. I've wondered over the years why highly successful junior college coaches are bypassed in favor of assistant coaches from high profile Division I programs.

I was thrilled that Western Kentucky wanted someone like me. I replaced Jim Richards, who just wanted to be the golf coach at Western Kentucky. I really don't know why they selected me, other than the fact Eddie Sutton helped me get the job. After spending four seasons with Eddie Sutton at Arkansas, he felt that if I was going to make a move, it probably was time to act. The Western Kentucky selection committee liked my interview and enthusiasm. They seemed extremely interested that I would make myself available for alumni outings, which was important at that school.

I was attracted to the Western Kentucky job in part because they have a nice arena, and the basketball program had an excellent following. The Western Kentucky fans were great and continue to be great. I had a good feeling about all the people who were around me at the school.

Once on campus, I adapted easily to the community in Bowling Green, Kentucky. At that time, I was a jogger and began jogging with a judge. I also became part of a morning coffee group, along with guys who also had been friends of Ed

Diddle, the former coach there and quite a character. The athletic director was John Oldham, who had played basketball in the NBA with the Fort Wayne Pistons. One of Oldham's teammates with the Pistons was Fred Schaus, who coached Purdue during the mid-'70s and was on staff at Purdue when I took over in 1980.

As I prepared for my first season at Western Kentucky, I was elated to be coaching Division I basketball. There were times when I almost couldn't believe it. That feeling was very much like the one I experienced after winning a Big Ten championship at Purdue. As I thought back about the Idaho State job after I had moved onto Western Kentucky, I was pleased that I had been selective in my Division I coaching opportunities. I think that whenever possible, a coach needs to pick a position at a place that has tradition. In my case, Western Kentucky had lots of basketball tradition. Idaho State did not have that same tradition.

My first season at Western Kentucky was memorable. We finished 17-11 and really won the Ohio Valley Tournament championship, but a referee called a foul seconds after the game was over. We were leading Eastern Kentucky by one point, and they allowed the opponent to shoot both free throws, which were made. A special league hearing was called on the following Monday with both athletic directors, the Ohio Valley commissioner and the league's supervisor of officials.

We really won that game, but the NCAA stepped in and ruled that because each team left the tournament championship venue and that the scorebook had been signed, the victory was awarded to Eastern Kentucky. Until the NCAA tournament of 2005, Eastern Kentucky had not made an NCAA

**I was disappointed to lose to Virginia Tech in the 1980 NCAA tournament, but overall my two seasons at Western Kentucky were a success.**
*Sports Information Department of Western Kentucky University*

tournament appearance since 1979. TV camera footage and photographs documented proof that we had won that game, but the decision did not go in our favor.

In 1979, we were more determined than ever at Western Kentucky to win the Ohio Valley tournament. One of the best players on the 1979 team was Curtis Townsend, who now is an assistant coach at Kansas. It was a team that had good depth, and with Clem Haskins as my assistant coach, it was a lot of fun. Ray Hite, who had played at North Carolina for Dean Smith, was another of my Western Kentucky assistants.

That Western Kentucky team was successful in large part because we were a patient team. It's funny, because the radio play-by-play announcer there didn't like the way we played. In the past, Western Kentucky featured a run-and-gun style. But we were successful because we did what we could do well, and not what a radio announcer or some fans preferred.

In the NCAA tournament, we played Virginia Tech and built a 17-point halftime lead. However, we were unable to hold it and lost. Had we won that game, we would have played Bob Knight's Indiana team, which was led by freshman guard Isiah Thomas.

Losing is never a pleasant experience, but in that second season at Western Kentucky, we established a great sense of pride, which is what that program has been about.

During my two seasons at Western Kentucky, I earned a base salary of $24,000, plus $6,000 for a TV show. The other part of the arrangement was that if we made any profit from our summer basketball camp, I could keep that money.

For me, that was quite an improvement from that $15,000 a year I was making at Arkansas at the time I left to become the head coach at Western Kentucky. Little did I know that my career was about to experience the change of a lifetime.

## CHAPTER FIVE

# Next Stop, West Lafayette

After our Western Kentucky team was eliminated from the 1980 NCAA tournament, a friend of mine from Bowling Green, Dan Davis, asked me if I wanted to fly with him to Indianapolis to watch the 1980 Final Four, in which Purdue was a participant. Dan owned his own plane, and he and I flew to Indianapolis to watch Purdue play UCLA in one semifinal. Louisville and Iowa were the other two members of that Final Four. Our seats were in the top row at Market Square Arena, which now is demolished. As Dan and I sat and watched UCLA beat Purdue, I had no idea that I would become the next Purdue coach. It was irony at its best.

Lee Rose was the Purdue coach during the 1979-80 season, after which he resigned to take the University of South Florida job in Tampa. Suddenly, Purdue was in need of a coach. Fred Schaus, who had coached the Boilermakers in the '70s, was on the Purdue staff in 1980. He had seen me coach a National Sports Festival team in Colorado Springs in the summer of 1979 and was impressed, so he contacted athletic director John Oldham at Western Kentucky. Honestly, I think Oldham wanted Purdue to take me. He thought that I was too active along the sideline during games. I believe he wanted a calmer coach to replace me, but I think he got fooled when he hired Clem Haskins as my replacement.

When Rose left Purdue, George King, who was athletic director at that time, called me and asked if I would be interested in interviewing. Purdue flew me to West Lafayette. I was one of four potential replacements for Rose. I don't know if I came into the Purdue interview as the leading candidate, but during the interview I focused on just being myself. I explained to the search committee that I would do anything that was asked of me in terms of helping with alumni functions and making myself available for public appearances. I also shared with them that recruiting would be my No. 1 priority. I expressed that Mackey Arena is a great place to play and that as a member of the Big Ten Conference, Purdue was in a very special basketball league. At that time, the Big Ten had one of the few strong television packages in college basketball. I told the search committee members that Purdue was a great opportunity for a guy who was looking to do something very special with his coaching career. But when all was said and done, I think my willingness to be involved in alumni activities impressed the people who were making the decision. I walked away from my interview feeling as if it went well. I don't think I could have done any better. I wanted the Purdue job, and I thought I positioned myself to get it.

To this day, people have attempted to make a big deal out of the fact that I took over at Purdue during the time that Bob Knight's Indiana teams were excellent. But the fact that Bob was the coach at Purdue's main rival never was a factor to me as I weighed the pros and cons of becoming Purdue's next coach. To me, it was a great opportunity to be able to coach against someone like Bob Knight. At the time, I really respected him as a coach, and I didn't know him as a person. My only interaction with Bob Knight had taken place when I was an assistant at Arkansas, and Bob, Eddie Sutton, and I attended a clinic together in Tulsa. Bob was the featured speaker at the clinic, and the three of us drove back to Fayetteville, Arkansas, together because Bob wanted Eddie to take him fishing. The next year, Eddie got mad at our Arkansas team and threw the players out of practice, after which Eddie and I boarded a school plane and flew to Bloomington, Indiana, to watch the Hoosiers practice.

I'm older than Bob, but I was in awe of the man. Actually, I felt like I was younger than he was, especially in spirit. But when I became the Purdue coach, I never gave any consideration to those who said that Indiana was his state. I probably wasn't that smart. I just thought Purdue offered a great opportunity to coach for a school that had a great tradition. John Wooden, Rick Mount, Terry Dischinger, Dave Schellhase—those were great basketball players in a state that adores this sport.

I also sensed that I would be surrounded by great people at Purdue. At that time, two of Purdue's former star quarterbacks—Bob DeMoss and Dale Samuels—were athletic administrators, and I admired them very much. Thanks to all of the summer alumni outings that Purdue stages, I got to know Bob and Dale extremely well on the golf course. I was not a good golfer when I arrived at Purdue—I was a jogger and a tennis player instead—and I worried that I would never become as talented on the golf course as those guys. I hoped that I would not tarnish my standing among Purdue alumni with a poor showing on the golf course.

But as I became familiar with everyone from the maintenance crew in Ross-Ade Stadium to all those who worked in Mackey Arena, I quickly realized that Gene Keady and Purdue would become a good fit. My contract also was a good fit. It was April, 1980, and I was making a base salary of $42,000. With TV and radio shows, my initial compensation package at Purdue was right at $60,000.

As I balanced alumni outings and learning the community, I began to build our Purdue basketball program upon my arrival. Even during the interview process, I thought about what the 1980-81 team might be like. Forward Drake Morris and guards Keith Edmondson and Brian Walker would return from the 1979-80 Final Four team, but center Joe Barry Carroll, who was the heart of that team, and power forward Arnette Hallman were graduating. I knew that if we were going to compete in the rugged Big Ten, we needed immediate help. Our first big signee was Russell Cross, an excellent center from Chicago. We also signed Greg Eifert, a forward from Fort Wayne, and Ricky Hall, an unheralded guard from Fort Wayne. Curt Clawson, another guard, came to us after serving a Mormon mission, and yet another guard, Steve Reid, transferred from Kansas State. Certainly, we didn't know it at the

**My first coaching staff at Purdue included (left to right) Clarence Glover, Jay Williams, and Bruce Weber.** *Purdue Sports Information*

time, but we quickly had put into place the key pieces to what would become the 1984 Big Ten championship team.

✦ ✦ ✦ ✦

As I prepared for the 1980-81 season, I realized that the challenge would be meshing the old with the new. I was new, along with my first recruiting class. The old centered on those players who had experienced a Final Four playing for Coach Rose and were accustomed to his methods. It was a pretty good team, but we never developed great chemistry, in part because I never got the impression that the players really liked each other or enjoyed each other's company. It was a team that never really clicked.

I did not recruit the upperclassmen, and often, older players resent any situation involving a new coach. Kevin Stallings, now the coach at Vanderbilt, was among the best-known members of my first team. We had a shared history before my arrival, because I had attempted to recruit Kevin to Arkansas when he was a high school player in Collinsville, Illinois. Kevin was not fun to coach. He is a good guy, and I like him very much; but while I thought Kevin would be a very good coach, as a player he was not as talented as he thought he was. He thought that he was an excellent shooter. In truth, he wasn't that bad, but he wasn't great, either. Plus, his slow feet plagued him. But he was a much better passer and an excellent student of the game. I figured that he was well suited to some day enter the coaching profession. In recent years, Kevin and I have shared a lot of laughs about my observations of him as a player. Now, he says, "You are right, Coach." During all the years he has been a head coach—first at Illinois State and then at Vanderbilt—he has had an opportunity to coach players who were exactly like him when he was a player.

As for that team's core group, Russell Cross was my center and was a good guy to go to, because Russell took the pressure off Keith Edmonson, who was our starting shooting guard. Small forward Drake Morris, who played at tradition-rich East Chicago Washington High School, was a very good player as well. Brian Walker was my point guard and was a very positive person. Before one of our road trips, I told the team that I thought it would be a successful trip if we could split the two games. Brian, who was an Indiana All-Star from Lebanon High School, was angry that I would consider a two-game split successful. Brian said, "We're going to win both games, Coach." I liked that sort of attitude from my players.

We were 11-3 through a January victory against Northwestern before going 6-7 in our final 13 Big Ten Conference games to finish the regular season at 17-10, which was good enough for a National Invitation Tournament berth. That initial postseason experience was excellent, because we had the opportunity to play five more games, including three in Mackey Arena, where we defeated Rhode Island, Dayton, and Duke to qualify for the Final Four in New York City's Madison Square Garden.

After losing to Syracuse in the semifinals, the highlight of our trip to New York came in defeating West Virginia—coached by Gale Catlett—75-72 in overtime in the third-place match. I had a lot of respect for Gale, because when I was coaching at Hutchinson Junior College, Gale was an assistant coach at Kansas. To beat Gale Catlett was a big deal, but our players did not know I thought that. Overall, I think the NIT that year was good for our freshmen, because they had an opportunity to experience a high level of competition in the bright lights of New York City.

After my first season at Purdue, I tried not to analyze the results too much. I was just trying to keep my job. I've always been one of those coaches who thinks, "I've got to do a good job this year, so that I can keep my job next year." We had finished my first season 21-11, and I remember thinking that I certainly was lucky to have this job. I never, ever thought that any school was lucky to have Gene Keady coaching their team.

We used the 21-11 record and the trip to the NIT's Final Four to land Michigan City's Dan Palombizio, who was Indiana's Mr. Basketball. At that time, I did not realize what a great accomplishment it was to sign a Mr. Basketball. The downside of that recruiting success was that Palombizio turned out to be a player who was not team-oriented. He ended up leaving our program and transferring to Ball State, where he did well.

During the 1981-82 season, we went to the NIT Final Four again and lost to Bradley, 67-58, in the championship game. In all of the recruiting letters that I sent out after the 1981-82 season, I wrote that we had been to the Final Four two years in a row. We used that as a recruiting gimmick.

✦ ✦ ✦ ✦

Before he left our program, Dan Palombizio was among the players who helped us take the next step during the 1982-83 season, when we earned our first NCAA Tournament berth in my tenure. That was an interesting team, because for much of the season we struggled to identify ourselves. Yet when the regular season ended, we were 20-8, including two victories against Illinois and a triple-overtime victory at Michigan. We

**We had plenty to celebrate in my third season, 1982-83, including a 56-54 win over Illinois at the Assembly Hall that helped to ensure our bid to the NCAA tournament.** *Purdue Sports Information*

were 10-1 at one point that year and then went 5-2 during our final seven Big Ten Conference games. That was enough to impress the NCAA tournament selection committee, which extended a bid our way.

In the NCAA, we were placed in the Mideast Regional in Tampa. We opened with a 55-53 victory against Robert Morris, thanks to a Steve Reid game-winning shot. That was a difficult game for us, because none of our players were familiar with Robert Morris, which just two years before had been a junior college. I remember telling our players, "These guys can play!" Robert Morris was a quick team that was very good defensively. We were facing them without our center, Russell Cross, who was nursing a knee injury, and our point guard, Ricky Hall, who was battling the flu. Operating at less than 100 percent, our play suffered. This game was played in the era before the 35-second shot clock, so we held the ball for the final three minutes, setting up a final shot that Reid hit to win that game.

Beating Robert Morris was a good-news, bad-news scenario for me, because by virtue of advancing into the second round, we would play Arkansas and my mentor, coach Eddie Sutton. He was the last guy who I wanted to play. Plus, that Arkansas team included three players who, in my opinion, had NBA talent. Arkansas was ranked ninth nationally at the time, and they beat us 78-68. We hung with them throughout most of the game, but Coach Sutton and his staff had done an excellent job scouting us. His team made several key steals off our guard-to-forward pass. It seemed as if each time we wanted to enter the basketball to the forward, Arkansas made steals coming off the wing. But I was proud that we were able to hurt them inside, getting a lot of layups from Russell Cross.

It was disappointing to lose to Eddie and Arkansas, but they probably should have beaten us, because they had better players than we did. I have always admired Eddie's teams, because much like John Wooden's great UCLA teams, they are extremely disciplined and play good, fundamental basketball. Their team defense is superb, and they will not beat themselves by attempting bad shots. That was the case in our 1983 NCAA tournament loss to Arkansas.

## CHAPTER SIX

# Turning the Corner

The 1983-84 season was the springboard that enabled me to remain at Purdue for 25 years, while at the same time assuring me that I would complete my coaching career at the Division I level. The irony is that I really did not see a 22-7 record, a Big Ten Conference championship, and a trip to the NCAA tournament as a possibility for that team. Certainly, our team chemistry was excellent. But what I did not realize at the start of the season was that those players had absorbed the points of emphasis stressed by our coaching staff. That team attempted to do everything they were told.

Seniors Jim Rowinski, Ricky Hall, Curt Clawson, and Greg Eifert comprised the core of that Big Ten championship team. One of the key elements that facilitated everything coming together was Clawson's willingness to accept his role as a reserve player. During the 1982-83 season, Curt, a guard-forward, was a starter. He became a crowd favorite during the 1982 exhibition season when he sank a shot from the corner to defeat one of the Soviet Union's finest traveling teams, 66-65.

After Curt's junior year, we recruited Mark Atkinson, a 6-7 junior college player who was from Brownsburg, Indiana. Mark was a scorer who hit 57.7 percent from the field that year and averaged 8.1 points. He was a more talented player than Curt, so naturally we moved Mark into the starting lineup ahead of Curt. Thankfully, Curt did not take it personally. Instead, he encouraged the other four members of what would be our second unit to become an extremely competitive group. We had excellent depth in Mack Gadis, Herb Robinson, James Bullock, and Steve Reid. Every day in practice I could count on a high level of competition, and I owe a lot of that to Curt Clawson's wonderful attitude. Thanks to him, we really improved as a team.

That year we took extremely good care of the basketball, averaging only 9.9 turnovers a game. We also shot free throws well and made almost 50 percent of our attempts from the field. There was no three-point line at that time, so obviously, it was easier for a team to shoot a higher percentage from the floor. Another key to our success was the development of Rowinski, a 6-8, 200-pound center. Rowinski had come to Purdue as a walk-on under Lee Rose, and when I took over for the 1980-81 season, he walked on for us, too. Jim continued to get a little bit better and then a little bit better, while at the same time continuing to grow. He was 6-4 when he joined Lee Rose's team. Like former Michigan standout Roy Tarpley,

Much of our success in 1983-84 was due to Curt Clawson's willingness to accept a demotion to a reserve role. He helped to make our practices competitive by energizing our second unit. *Purdue Sports Information*

Rowinski was one of those kids who continued growing throughout college. The Michigan coaches told me that Tarpley grew six inches during the time he was a Wolverine.

Jim was one of those kids who just loved to play basketball. In his first three seasons playing for me, he scored a total of 108 points in 36 ballgames. Then, in 1983-84, Rowinski averaged 15 points and 6.7 rebounds, shooting 50 percent from the field and 76.5 percent from the free throw line. I have to give him a lot of credit for his desire to make the most of an opportunity. In 1980-81, he suffered a broken foot in a game against Houston in the Sugar Bowl Classic. But he battled back from that, dedicating himself to rehab and then getting stronger in our weight room. He began to become such a dedicated lifter that I started calling him, "Mr. Beach," because he had the look of one of those body-builders you often see at a beach. By the time Jim was a senior, his body was huge, he had improved his strength and he had worked on his shot. He became a very difficult matchup for any opponent.

During that era of college basketball, not many teams were as physical as Purdue was on the court. Throughout that season, everyone on the team bought into playing with passion, and to a man, they played above their potential. That identity—of playing passionate, physical ball—became our secret to success during the next 20 years.

We began the season at the Sun-Met Classic in Fresno, California, and defeated Fresno State 56-55 in the championship game. We fed off that victory and were 7-0 and ranked 11th in the nation when we entered a three-game sequence in December at Evansville, at DePaul and versus Kentucky in Louisville. We lost those three games by 41 combined points, which probably caused people to overlook us. Then we

**Jim Rowinski—also known as "Mr. Beach"—blossomed during his senior season, averaging 15 points and nearly seven rebounds per game.**

*Purdue Sports Information*

bounced right back and won 10 of our first 11 Big Ten games, including an eight-point victory at Indiana in January. At that point, people began to take notice once again.

We jumped back into the rankings, despite the fact that the team did not have any NBA-type players on its roster. But people appreciated how hard those kids played, and people liked me and the way that I coached. I don't want to downplay our talent, because we had some excellent players at Purdue, but throughout the years we probably were often rewarded in the NCAA tournament with a better seed than we deserved. Maybe we weren't really as talented as the teams that we were seeded alongside. I don't want to say this in a derogatory fashion, but when kids play so hard, sometimes they are rewarded for those efforts.

In 1983-84, we were 14-3 in the Big Ten race when we traveled to Minnesota for a game on March 10. A victory would give us the Big Ten title, but until that day, my previous teams had always struggled when playing at Minnesota. The Gophers featured big, strong forwards, and I remember thinking, "We will never beat these guys. They are too good for us." A normal fan would have compared our teams and agreed with me. Maybe Minnesota's players thought that way as well, which worked in our favor.

Another factor heading into that final game was that in that era, the Big Ten used a traveling-partner system, and our traveling partner was Illinois. Illinois would go into a place on Thursday night—say Minnesota, for example—and beat up on that team. Then, we would come in on Saturday or Sunday and upset a team that was not ready for us. We helped Illinois, too, because we would physically beat up a team on Thursday, and then Illinois would beat that team on Saturday. In a way, we had a great relationship with Illinois.

The two of us ended up sharing the Big Ten championship after we beat Minnesota 63-62 in the final regular season. The game was nationally televised, and we got a combined 30 points and 15 rebounds from Rowinski and Atkinson. We led 32-27 at halftime and barely held them off down the stretch. It truly was a great game. A key for us was that we put in some special stunts for free-throw situations when we were shooting them. We would set screens in case a free throw came off the rim short. Another stunt was to have two players go in behind their players who were closest to the basket. Sure enough, with 45 seconds remaining, we had a two-point lead with Steve Reid—one of our best free-throw shooters—going to the line. We thought Steve would make the free throw, but it was short. Taking advantage of one of our stunts, Ricky Hall used his quickness to rebound the ball and dribble it away from trouble. That is how we saved the game.

We flew home from Minneapolis that night anxious to learn where we would be sent for the NCAA tournament's opening round. On the way home, we got word on the plane that we were in the Midwest Regional and were going to play against Memphis State, which featured Keith Lee and Baskerville Holmes as its stars. We won the Big Ten championship and then enjoyed two hours of joy before learning that our reward for that championship was a date with Memphis State on their home floor in Memphis. I remember thinking, "What the hell? Why is the NCAA mad at a Big Ten team?"

But there really was a lot more than two hours of joy. When we returned to campus that night, a crowd estimated at between 4,000 and 5,000 was there to greet us as we pulled in front of Mackey Arena. During my 25 seasons at Purdue, we often were greeted by our fans, but that turnout—for a team the media picked to finish last in the Big Ten—was a tremendous indication of how much our efforts were appreciated.

We prepared for the NCAA trip to Memphis, but we simply did not shoot well enough to beat an extremely talented Memphis State team. We shot less than 30 percent from the field and were beaten 66-48. That wasn't the ending we sought, but in no way did one loss diminish what our 1983-84 team had accomplished. Before that season, some Purdue fans probably wondered why I had been selected in 1980 to guide this basketball program. But during that wonderful season, those very same fans began to embrace our program.

✦ ✦ ✦ ✦

Thanks in large part to the success we experienced during the 1983-84 season, we landed a recruiting class that remains the favorite of many Purdue fans: shooting guard Troy Lewis, forward Todd Mitchell, and point guard Everette Stephens. Beginning with the 1984-85 season, and continuing through the completion of the 1987-88 season, Troy, Todd, and Everette led us to a record of 96-28, including Big Ten championships in 1987 and 1988. When the trio was juniors and seniors, we went a combined 54-9 and were ranked no lower than 13th in any weekly poll.

I recruited Troy the hardest because he is from Anderson, Indiana, which is less than two hours east of West Lafayette. I can tell you that I wore out the roads that lead from West Lafayette to Anderson. I became good friends with Norm Held, who was the Anderson High School coach, and I think that helped me win Troy over. To this day, Norm and I are good friends and golf buddies.

So with Troy, it was a matter of driving back and forth from the campus of Purdue to Anderson to visit him. During the time Troy played there, Anderson High School had a great team. He took Anderson to the Indiana high school state finals championship game in 1983 and lost to Connersville by one point. In 1984, when Troy was a senior, Anderson was ranked No. 1 most of the year before losing to Lake Central in the Lafayette Semistate, which was played in Mackey Arena.

While I saw Troy play frequently, I recruited Todd more by phone, because he was so far away in Toledo, Ohio. I'm not the kind of coach who will leave practice to drive somewhere to watch a high school game. A lot of coaches leave practices for recruiting purposes and let their assistant coaches direct the remainder of practice, but I never did that sort of thing. In the end, I think we got Todd because Troy decided to come to Purdue. Todd always wanted to play college basketball with Troy.

We nabbed Everette because I told him he was going to go to Purdue. We were sitting in the car, and I said, "Everette, sign this. You are going to Purdue." Seriously, that's about how quickly things moved and how easy his recruitment was to complete. It was between Purdue and Kentucky, and I think he liked that I told him I was going to convert him into a point guard, since he played small forward in high school.

The other thing that helped us with Everette was that his sister-in-law was legendary baseball player Minnie Minoso's daughter. Minnie was a great player for the Chicago White Sox in the 1950s, and Everette is from the Chicago suburb of Evanston. Everette's sister-in-law sat in on our recruiting meeting and liked what I had to say. She helped us sign Everette, along with his parents.

A key to landing all three of them was that each came from a very solid family. Each of those three young men had a great mother. I like Todd's dad, too. When I visited their home to sign Todd, his father looked at me and said, "I'm not signing anything with you unless you have a shot of bourbon with me." So as we signed the letter of intent, his father and I each had a shot of bourbon. But I've always said the key to recruiting is that you have to sell the player's mother on what her son is going to be doing for the next four or five years of his life. I always stressed—and with Troy, Todd, and Everette it was no different—that at Purdue, we are going to be a basketball family. I told them that their son would get a degree. I told them that with our excellent coaching staff, their son would become a better player.

In 1984, the NBA wasn't the great selling point to potential recruits that it is today. Twenty years ago, parents weren't worried about whether or not their sons would play in the NBA; instead, parents were concerned with their sons earning a college degree. Amateur Athletic Union basketball also wasn't a factor in the recruiting process 20 years ago.

In today's basketball environment, had Troy, Todd, or Everette been a part of the AAU culture, we may not have gotten them to come to Purdue. In fact, after Troy had been on our campus for three months in the fall of 1984, he said that he wished he had signed with Kansas because we ran our players so much during conditioning. Obviously, Troy adjusted, and along with Todd and Everette, formed one of the best trios ever to play at Purdue. Through the 2004-05 season, Troy ranks fourth on the school's career scoring list with 2,038

**Landing (left to right) Troy Lewis, Todd Mitchell, and Everette Stephens in the same recruiting class put a big smile on my face.** *Purdue Sports Information*

points, Todd is ninth with 1,699, and Everette ranks 37th with 1,044.

There were many contributing factors to the program's success during the Troy, Todd, and Everette era. For starters, I know that basketball was the most important thing to them, which was a quality that my Purdue teams lacked during the final five years of my tenure. The three of them were fun to coach because they did not have big egos—they just wanted to win. Each one of them would tape the game, and when they went home at night, they would watch the game. The next day, when we would come in for our scouting report and analysis of how we had performed, they already were ahead of the coaching staff.

When those three played here, Sundays were big days for us. At that time, we were not mandated by the NCAA to take a day off, which is the case now. If we played on a Saturday, we would bring the team in on Sunday to watch the game tape, lift weights, and go for a team swim in the old Lambert Fieldhouse pool. Swimming helped to bring the team together, because instead of making it a simple recreational pleasure, we would also have competitive races and relays. Half the guys on those teams didn't know how to swim when they were freshmen. They would learn to swim, and then it became fun for them.

I was very upset when the NCAA passed legislation that forced us to take a day off. It destroyed that bonding experience that we developed when we could bring our teams in on Sundays. And we still gave the players a day off, if needed— but it was of our choosing. Say it was the middle of January, and the players were a little tired. We would give them a day off when they did not know it was coming, and that fired them up. They would come in ready to go when we practiced the day after. We lost some of the edge we had during that era when the NCAA stepped in and told coaches that we didn't know what we were doing. The NCAA was afraid that we wouldn't give players a day off, and that we would work them too hard or take away from their study time.

For a program such as Purdue, a mandated day off is not good. To win here, players must be good students, and they must have an excellent work ethic. Purdue probably isn't going

**As they say, practice does make perfect. I was upset when the NCAA forced programs to take a day off during the week.** *Purdue Sports Information*

to sign a lot of McDonald's All-Americans. So, the players and coaches have to work that much harder. Troy, Todd, and Everette worked hard, and they did so without a mandated day off.

✦ ✦ ✦ ✦

Not long into practice for the 1984-85 season, I realized that the three freshmen—Troy, Todd, and Everette—were going to provide additional, immediate firepower to comple-

**As a freshman, all that forward Todd Mitchell wanted to do was dunk the ball. But by the time he graduated he became a complete player.**
*Purdue Sports Information*

ment a solid group of players returning from the 1984 Big Ten championship team. Troy was athletic and an excellent shooter. Everette displayed an ability to play the point, get to the rim, and guard people. It was a bonus to have a point guard who had shot-blocking skills. Todd's only problem was that he did not like to guard. As a freshman, he just wanted to dunk. I remember a conversation with Todd early in his freshman season in which I told him, "I don't care what you think of me, because I'm going to work you on defense until I make you into an All-Big Ten selection." And I did. Todd and I had several disagreements, but it never was personal. He's always been a great person, and he is a good friend now.

Those three blended nicely with seniors Steve Reid, Jim Bullock, and Mark Atkinson and junior Mack Gadis. Mack was a solid player, but I frequently had to remind him to keep his weight down. Doug Lee, Herb Robinson, and Tim Fisher also were important to us during the 1984-85 season. They were mature, intelligent players. Fisher, who now is a doctor, wasn't concerned about playing time. He was happy to be a member of the team and help us in any way he could.

The 1984-85 team played well early in the season, winning nine of its first 10 games, including a win over Kentucky. And the game we lost—an 84-79 loss to Miami (Ohio)—was in Mackey Arena. We beat Mississippi State and Texas-El Paso in the Sun Bowl Classic to cap a 9-1 non-conference portion of our schedule. As we began our defense of our Big Ten championship, we started poorly, losing three of our first four including back-to-back home games to Michigan State (in overtime) and to Michigan. We rallied to go 10-4 down the stretch in conference play, which was good enough for a return trip to the NCAA tournament.

We were assigned to opening-round games in the Southeast Regional at South Bend, Indiana. But in round one we drew Auburn, which was led by Chuck Person. Person was incredibly talented and went on to enjoy a fine NBA career. We played relatively well, but Auburn beat us 59-58, marking the second straight year we were defeated in the opening round of the tournament.

Our 1985-86 team was another that performed very well in non-conference competition, going 11-2 before the start of Big Ten play. No. 1-ranked North Carolina and No. 16-ranked Louisville were our only losses before league action. We started the 1986 Big Ten season with a 76-73 overtime victory against Iowa. Six games into the Big Ten schedule, our record stood at 16-3 and we were ranked 15th in the nation. But beginning with a one-point, overtime loss at Indiana, we experienced a four-game losing streak. After the loss at IU, we also were beaten by Ohio State, Illinois, and Michigan, which essentially removed us from the Big Ten title chase.

We followed the four-game losing streak with a five-game winning streak, however, which included an 85-68 victory against Indiana—ranked 15th at the time—in Mackey Arena. We completed our regular season with a 22-9 mark, which secured our fourth straight berth in the NCAA tourney. But for the second time in three seasons, we ended up playing an opening-round NCAA tournament game on our opponent's court. And for the third time in a row, we dropped our opening game. LSU beat us 94-87 in double overtime on their way to the Final Four. That was the last year in which games were played on a team's home court in the NCAA men's tournament.

The score was tied near the end of regulation, so we set up a play for Troy. We ran the play perfectly; Troy had a wide-open shot, but he missed it. LSU's point guard also played the bulk of the second half with four fouls, and while he continued to foul us, nothing was called against him. We didn't get any breaks in that game, and to win in the NCAA tournament you have to get those kinds of breaks.

✦ ✦ ✦ ✦

While I was frustrated by what happened to us in the loss to LSU—playing on their court and not catching a single break—I took consolation in the fact that our 1986-87 team had the potential to be very good. Now, Troy, Todd, and Everette were junior starters, and they were surrounded by pretty good talent. Melvin McCants, our center, had played well as a freshman in 1985-86, and Doug Lee was a senior small forward who rounded out our starting five. We had good size and exceptional athletes. And we had good shooters, too. Clearly, this was a solid team. It might have even been our best team during my tenure.

After starting the season 14-1, we were still sailing along at 24-3 and ranked No. 3 in the nation when we went to Michigan for our regular-season finale. Michigan beat the heck out of us, 104-68. While we were still Big Ten champs and finished the season ranked seventh, the NCAA tournament selection committee assigned us to the East Regional in Syracuse, New York, while it sent Indiana to Indianapolis to play in the RCA Dome. The Hoosiers went on to win the NCAA championship, beating Syracuse in New Orleans. Had we not lost so badly at Michigan, I'm pretty sure that Indiana would have been assigned to Syracuse, and we would have received the trip to Indianapolis. It seems like when it came to Purdue and the NCAA tournament, it was always something—an injury, a tough loss, you name it. But that's life, so we went to Syracuse, which became a unique trip for us, to say the least.

Purdue athletic trainer Denny Miller had lived in Syracuse briefly and told me that our team absolutely had to stay downtown at the Syracuse Hotel, which was a popular place with lots of tradition. What Denny failed to mention was that we were going to be in Syracuse during St. Patrick's Day festivities, and that there are many Irish in the Syracuse area. Our team's rooms were on the 12th floor, and we couldn't get to them. It was estimated that there were as many as 8,000 people in or around the Syracuse Hotel on St. Patrick's Day, and we could not get on an elevator because so many people were using it. It was just nuts. We had beaten Northeastern in the opening round of the tournament and were trying to come back to the hotel and get ready for our second-round game against Florida. I remember turning to the others in our party and saying, "Damn, I wish we weren't staying here." The only way we could get to our rooms was to walk the full 12 flights of stairs.

I've always told my players at every level that I've coached to expect the unexpected. But to this day, I don't know how you tell your players to deal with 8,000 crazy people who are partying on St. Patrick's Day. There was nothing we could do to change the environment, because all of the city's other hotels were booked with teams and fans there to watch the NCAA tournament games. We could not change hotels. We should have followed the lead of Georgetown coach John Thompson, who always housed his teams at least an hour from the NCAA tournament site.

Staying at the Syracuse Hotel was distracting and frustrating, but it's not the reason that we lost to Florida, 85-66. The truth was Florida had one hell of a team with Dwayne Schintzius and Vernon Maxwell and their talented bench also hurt us. During the game, Maxwell spit in a couple of our players' faces, and then Doug Lee, who had shot the ball so well against Northeastern, could not buy a basket. Florida featured some very good athletes, and they guarded us well. It was a good lesson for our team, because it taught us that you have to play, regardless of the circumstances. Needless to say, the circumstances we encountered in Syracuse were among the strangest in my association with basketball.

## CHAPTER SEVEN

# From Top to Bottom

**R**un and gun. That's what we planned to do a lot of during the 1987-88 season, when Troy Lewis, Todd Mitchell, and Everette Stephens were seniors. We scored 100 points in an exhibition game victory against the Czechs and then opened the regular season with a 102-88 triumph against Arkansas-Little Rock in the preseason National Invitation Tournament in Mackey Arena. We were ranked second in the nation as we prepared to play Iowa State in the NIT quarterfinals in Mackey. One more victory would send us to New York's Madison Square Garden for the NIT's Final Four. But our run-and-gun plan went up in smoke when Iowa State beat us 104-96. So much for all offense and no defense. Troy Lewis said the three practices we had in the aftermath of the loss to Iowa State were the toughest he ever experienced. We returned to a premise of defense. In our next game, we traveled to Illinois State and won, 68-61. Then we followed it up with a victory at Wichita State, and we were off and running in what would become a 29-4 season that included our second consecutive Big Ten championship.

The loss to Iowa State became an excellent learning tool in that it got our players' attention regarding shot selection. Our coaching staff adjusted its philosophy from running and gunning to playing the way we were accustomed to playing, which centered on stopping people and taking the best available shot. One of the misperceptions that we constantly battled was that a Keady-coached team was going to be a slow-the-ball-down team.

Some opposing coaches would tell players we were recruiting that we were a slow-tempo team. They would tell kids, "You're not going to enjoy playing in Coach Keady's system, because everything is going to be about defense." Coaches used that tactic against us, so in 1987-88 we were trying to get some offense established in order to help our recruiting. But that attempt was a mistake. We just needed to keep winning, regardless of the method.

After the loss to Iowa State, we did win—16 in a row, in fact. I've always stressed playing at what I call "The Magic Level," and the 1987-88 team played at that level for several weeks. With just two games to go in Big Ten play, we were 15-1 with our only loss coming by three points at Indiana. We had a chance to finish 17-1 in Big Ten play, but we lost the next-to-last conference game at Ohio State, 71-60, for a 16-2 league

**Our game plan in 1987-88 was to run and gun with seniors like Troy Lewis. That strategy only lasted two games, and then our focus returned to defense.**
*Purdue Sports Information*

record. That loss dropped our season-ending national ranking from second to third in the poll.

Even with the loss at Ohio State, we had a tremendous Big Ten season. Troy, Todd, and Everette had gotten a lot stronger, and Melvin McCants and Kip Jones, who were underclassmen, had also improved. Our team featured very good depth with guard Tony Jones and center Steve Scheffler coming off the bench. Anytime a team has older kids, good athletes, and lots of depth, it has the makings for an excellent team. The other essential ingredient for us was that this team was comprised of players who had good attitudes. For most of the regular season, this was an exceptional team.

That excellence continued during the first and second rounds of the NCAA tournament in the Midwest Regional at South Bend, Indiana. We beat Farleigh Dickinson 94-79 and Memphis State 100-73 to earn a trip to the Sweet Sixteen in Pontiac, Michigan. Our next opponent was my alma mater, 20th-ranked Kansas State, a team we had beaten 101-72 in December in Mackey Arena.

In the NCAA tournament, much of a team's success relies on matchups, especially in terms of how a team's style compares to that of its opponent, and how both teams are playing at that particular point in the season. Kansas State, which was led by Mitch Richmond, was playing very well in March. We started with a 10-0 run to start the game, and that shocked our players, because we had blown them out in Mackey. In the December game, Richmond fouled out during the first half. But he didn't foul out this time. Most people considered us to be the better team, but Kansas State had some NBA talent and had improved significantly in January and February. They hit us with a 2-2-1 zone press and then settled back into a 1-2-2 zone. Lon Kruger, their coach at that time, has always been a good coach, and he had his team ready for us.

The game was close down the stretch, but in a key possession, Everette, who finished the game with 20 points, dribbled the ball off his foot for a turnover. Kansas State held on to beat us, 73-70. As I analyzed why we lost, I found that several things contributed. McCants had gotten into foul trouble, and we were without one of our big men backups in Jeff Arnold, who had left our program for personal reasons. Had we had Arnold as our backup center, that really would have helped us considering McCants foul problems. That was a bad break for us in terms of depth. In addition, Scheffler, who eventually became an excellent player for us, simply was not ready for the 1988 NCAA tournament. But we had to use him with Arnold not an option. During the game, he became nervous and hyperventilated. At that point in his career, he did not understand why it was important to go to the Final Four— a question he actually asked me once. Down the road, I took Steve with me to the 1989 World University Games, where he had an opportunity to play alongside Larry Johnson and Stacey Augmon of UNLV. Those two players helped Steve gain an appreciation for basketball, and encouraged him to establish his game. But that experience took place a year too late to help us in the 1988 NCAA tournament.

Of all the games that I've coached, I've never been as low as I was after Kansas State defeated us. I wanted to quit coaching and get out of the business. I allowed myself to believe that I was not a good enough coach. I said to people, "It's a damn shame that team didn't have a good enough coach to take them through this tournament." I felt very bad because

**Point guard Everette Stephens enjoyed a superb career at Purdue, finishing third on the school's career assists board with 481.** *Purdue Sports Information*

I was extremely close to all of those kids and their parents. Obviously, it was difficult to say goodbye to the senior members of our 1988 team.

My feelings about that game would slightly improve two or three years later when Mitch Richmond—who was selected fifth in the 1988 NBA draft—and his Kansas State teammate Steve Henson both made it in the NBA. None of our 1988 team members really made a splash in the NBA. I realized that Kansas State had better talent than we did, which caused me to feel just a little bit better. But it still doesn't mean that just because Kansas State had better talent than us, that we should have lost that game.

I was hoping that the success that Troy, Todd, and Everette experienced during four seasons at Purdue would carry over into the NBA, but Troy's feet were a little bit slow for the next level, and Todd at six foot six wasn't big enough to play forward in the NBA, although he made a lot of money playing professional basketball in Europe. Everette played one season with the Indiana Pacers, but sometimes his decision-making on the fastbreak was not the best. Deep inside, I knew the trio would have a difficult time making it as NBA players, even though to this day, Troy, Woody Austin, and his younger brother Chad Austin are the three finest shooters I ever coached.

✦ ✦ ✦ ✦

Coming off one of the finest basketball seasons in Purdue history, my ninth season as Boilermaker head coach was an extremely difficult experience. In 1988-89, we suddenly found ourselves with some very immature young men playing for us. From 1983—the first season in which every player in our program was someone my staff recruited—through 1988, our program had been all about being a basketball family. We were dedicated to becoming better year after year. We counted on our seniors to be the heart and soul of our team. But that was not the case in 1988-89.

We started out 6-3 after narrowly dropping our season opener in a rematch with Kansas State on their home floor. Then we struggled the rest of the season, finishing 15-16. I hated that Melvin McCants and Kip Jones—two kids who had been such important pieces of our 1986, '87 and '88 teams—had to go out with a losing record. We couldn't even play in the postseason NIT because we had a losing record. We won our final three regular-season games, but it wasn't enough. We suffered through a terrible sequence in January and February during which we lost seven of eight Big Ten games. And our senior leaders, Kip and Melvin, each experienced injuries during the season.

I didn't do us any favors by scheduling a game at Oregon on our way to the Rainbow Classic in Hawaii. Oregon sat back in a zone, and when we couldn't buy a basket they beat us 62-59. We went on to Hawaii, and after beating Southern California (68-64), we turned around and lost two more games to Hawaii and Georgia Tech by identical 72-69 scores. The team that had begun 6-3 was only 7-6 entering Big Ten play. Had we managed to beat either Oregon, Hawaii, or Georgia Tech, we would have finished the regular season 16-15 and certainly would have been invited to play in the NIT. As it worked out, our non-conference schedule was too difficult for that team.

The stretch of games at Oregon followed by three games in Hawaii should have made our team tougher, but it did not.

We had several bad apples on that basketball team who simply did not want to win. I don't mean that they were bad people. They were just "me" players instead of "team" players. But it is up to the coaches to get them to buy into the program and buy into a system—and we failed. Three of those "me" players—Loren Clyburn, Keith Stewart, and Billy Reid—left our program after the spring semester. In terms of talent, they were strong players. That's why we recruited them. But it was evident that they were more interested in personal gain than playing for the Purdue basketball family.

✦ ✦ ✦ ✦

Almost every Division I men's basketball coach evaluates himself, his program, and his career every so often, and after our defeat in the 1988 NCAA tournament followed by our first losing season at Purdue, I took a hard look at things. As I was evaluating where we had been and where we were headed, an opportunity to take over at Arizona State came my way in March 1989. Arizona State was a coaching position that I always wanted. My maternal grandfather and grandmother lived near Phoenix most of their lives, along with two of my uncles. In fact, one of my uncles was the principal at an Indian Reservation school for many years. I enjoyed lots of things about Arizona and always believed that Arizona State was a sleeping giant among college basketball's high-profile schools.

However, I did have concerns about the job. I wondered if the Phoenix area would support the NBA's Suns and a college program. I also was concerned about an NFL franchise—the Cardinals—that had recently moved to town competing for the fans' attention. And in talking with their athletic director, Charles Harris, he made it clear that he would not make improvements to our dressing room, nor did he want to create a room for entertaining alumni in the basketball arena. Those were elements I felt would be important to our success. Had we gotten some of those concessions, my wife, Pat, and I probably would have gone there.

Everyone probably will be amused by this, but the turning point in our decision did not center on basketball. In fact, at one point during our stay in the Phoenix area, I actually told the athletic director that I would take the job, although I did not sign anything. I really wanted to live in Arizona more than I wanted the Arizona State job. Pat and I got back on the jet and were flying to West Lafayette to inform everyone of our decision. We were in the air above one of the western states when I turned to her and said, "Have we made our final decision?" And she said, "I don't know ... it's awfully hot out there for our dogs." I said, "What? That's it. We're not going to Arizona State. If you are not going to say that we need to move and that we need to go to Arizona State, then I am not going." I guess Pat and I had our priorities in order. Our dogs were more important than getting another job.

I must admit that I found plenty about the Arizona State job to my liking. I was ready for the challenge. I liked the athletic director, with whom I had developed a friendship in 1988 when we played golf at La Costa Golf Resort in San Diego. The other appealing element was that Troy Young—my best friend in high school—was the athletic trainer at Arizona State. Troy, however, was not there during my interview, and that bothered me, because I wanted him there. I needed his support and his input as I faced a difficult decision. I walked away from the interview thinking, "How interested are they in having a good basketball program at Arizona State if they can't have my best friend involved in my interview?"

Pat and I were back home in Lafayette on Saturday night, and then-Michigan coach Bill Frieder called. Frieder asked me, "Are you going to accept the Arizona State job offer?" I said, "No," and Frieder's response was, "Hot dog, I'm out of here!" That's when Bill left Michigan to accept the job that I had turned down. Bo Schembechler, who was the Michigan athletic director at that time, was so upset that Frieder took the Arizona State job that he would not allow Bill to coach Michigan in the NCAA tournament that season. Steve Fisher, who was Bill's assistant, took over the Wolverine program and coached them to the 1989 NCAA tournament championship.

Within days of announcing that I would continue to coach the Boilermakers, I was very comfortable with my decision to stay. I had been so down about the 1988-89 season, but that's probably one reason I did not accept the Arizona State job. I did not want to leave the job at Purdue undone. I also really liked Steve Scheffler, Tony Jones, and Ryan Berning. I wanted to continue to coach them.

During the back-and-forth process with Purdue and Arizona State, I had a meeting with Dr. Steven Beering, who was the Purdue president at that time. I was in his office and happened to look out of a window. I noticed the architecture of the campus and all the red brick buildings and realized how fond I had become of the university. It struck me that Lafayette and West Lafayette comprised a natural campus setting, while Phoenix was a metropolitan area. Maybe I was dumb for passing up the offer, but I simply did not like Arizona State as well as I liked things at Purdue.

## CHAPTER EIGHT

# Back in the Hunt

I learned early on in my athletic career that the best way to deal with a frustrating loss or a losing season is to move on with energy and passion. After determining that I would not accept the Arizona State job, I jumped into preparing for the 1989-90 season, which proved to be an enjoyable year.

Center Steve Scheffler, guard Tony Jones, and forward Ryan Berning were my senior leaders, and they were all good players. We also had Jimmy Oliver, Chuckie White, Woody Austin, and Dave Barrett to go with them. And those "me" players from the year before had all left our program during the spring of 1989. As I observed this team during preseason practices, I thought we had a really good team, and as it turned out, we did. In fact, after beating Michigan 91-73 in late January in Ann Arbor, this team was 16-2 and ranked No. 8 in the nation. Unfortunately, we lost one-point games at Minnesota and Iowa and a two-pointer at Michigan State, or we would have won our third Big Ten championship in four seasons.

The key to that 22-8 season was the development of Scheffler. He and Tony Jones were members of the gold-medal-winning World University Games team that I took to Germany during the summer of 1989. On that trip, Scheffler listened as some great players explained to him why basketball is so important. They sold him on the importance of things such as footwork. He learned a great deal from the practice drills that were incorporated into the World University Games team's schedule. During his senior season, Scheffler responded by leading the nation in field goal percentage.

One of my favorite stories from the World University Games—and this tells you a lot about Scheffler—centers on a dunk that Steve had early in the gold medal game against the Soviet Union. He hung on the rim, and the glass absolutely shattered. He ran over to me and said, "Coach, I am so sorry." I said, "Steve, don't worry about it. They will put a new backboard in place." It took an hour, but they got it replaced.

With Steve having gained a lot of confidence that summer, we played well from the beginning of the season. Scheffler was extremely difficult to guard on the inside. Jimmy Oliver could shoot it. Chuckie White an excellent rebounder who would lead the Big Ten in rebounding the following year. Woody Austin gave us another lethal shooter. Craig Riley was a good backup center to Scheffler. And Tony Jones was an exceptional competitor who was not going to let

In the 1989-90 season, senior center Steve Scheffler proved to be a key as he was a tough assignment for opposing defenses. He finished the season averaging 16.8 points per game on nearly 70-percent shooting from the floor.

*Purdue Sports Information*

that team lose. Matt Painter, who replaced me as head coach at Purdue, also was a member of that team. We had depth, and we had what I like to refer to as "good basketball guys"— players who are driven and who have a strong desire to win.

However, we could have been even better had a strange scenario not played out while I was gone for three weeks with the World University Games team. Eddie Sutton had been let go by Kentucky, and his son, Sean, who was at Kentucky, was available. Sean committed to us and actually had gone so far as to move to West Lafayette and had rented an apartment. But Sean's mother didn't like our assistants and how they were handling all the details that go along with being a basketball player at Purdue. She wanted to know who picked the players' textbooks up for them. She was told that at Purdue, players are responsible for picking up their own textbooks. That did not please her. When I left for Germany, I told my assistant coaches, "The only thing you guys have to do during these next three weeks is make sure that Sean Sutton does not leave." He was a hell of a point guard and could have been the key to our 1989-90 team.

When I called the office to tell everyone the great news that we had won a gold medal, they told me that they had some bad news: Sutton was leaving Purdue. I was angry. With Sean, I'm sure we would have won the Big Ten and probably would have beaten Texas in the second round of the NCAA tournament. Sean ended up joining his father at Oklahoma State and was a hell of a player. In the end, it probably worked out best for him, but he certainly could have helped us, because Tony Jones was not a natural point guard. Tony played the position with some backup help from Dave Barrett, who I liked because he was an intense guy.

As I recall that season, I am reminded of how much our redshirt program helped us throughout the years at Purdue. Berning, for example, came to us in 1985 as a tall, skinny kid from Lafayette. We reshirted him, and he got much stronger and developed into a pretty good shooter. Through my first 20 years at Purdue, I was very proud that our players really improved and competed and were on the same page as the coaches.

The 1989-90 team was a perfect example of that philosophy. We had experienced a losing season the year before, but on the final day of the 1990 Big Ten season, we played at Michigan State with an opportunity to be champs. We were ranked 10th in the nation, and they were ranked seventh. We had a lead late in the game, but Michigan State fouled the hell out of us, stole the ball, and made a layup just ahead of the final buzzer to beat us 72-70. We finished 13-5 in the Big Ten with three of those five losses coming by a total of four points.

We entered the NCAA tournament ranked 10th in the final polls and were assigned to the Midwest Regional in Indianapolis, where we played first- and second-round games in the RCA Dome. We defeated Northeast Louisiana 75-63 in the opening round, setting up a game with Texas. That's a game that I never will forget. Unfortunately, it did not have a happy ending. Throughout the game, our players took six or seven charges, but the officiating crew would not actually call a charging foul on Texas. We lost 73-72, and when I entered our dressing room after the game, I was extremely frustrated by what had taken place. I saw Scheffler, Jones, and Berning sitting there crying, and that really upset me. In those days, the losing coach went to the mandated NCAA postgame press conference first, and I went berserk. I told everybody off.

When a coach has a display of unsportsmanlike conduct such as mine, that coach is required to go before an NCAA disciplinary committee during the Final Four. I had to appear before a group of people I knew well, including C.M. Newton, who coached for many seasons. During that hearing, they asked me, "What would you change to ensure that something like this does not happen to others?" I said that the losing coach should go second in the press conference format. The NCAA liked my idea and changed the sequence beginning the next season.

For the second time in my career at Purdue, I helped implement something known as "The Keady Rule." The first one—after we faced off against Memphis State and LSU on their home courts in the NCAA tournament—centered on not playing on an opponent's home court. The second "Keady Rule" made it possible for the losing coach in an NCAA tournament game to have extra time with his team, time that was needed to cool off before meeting the press.

If I would have been granted an additional 10 minutes to cool down and gather myself in the RCA Dome after our loss to Texas, I do not think I would have gone berserk. My wife probably would have gotten hold of me by then and reminded me to select my words carefully. That was as angry as I have ever been after a loss. No question about it. That response had been building up inside of me during the season. In a regular-season game at Iowa, we were defeated by one point on a fluke play, and then we lost in the closing seconds at Michigan State. After we lost to Texas by a point, I thought our kids deserved better. After my tirade, I received a $10,000 fine from the NCAA. Later, I learned that the guys who refereed the Texas game were good friends of then-Texas coach

Tom Penders. Had I known that, I probably would have received a $20,000 fine.

I paid a portion of the $10,000 fine, and George King, the Purdue athletic director who hired me to replace Lee Rose, helped pay a portion. In my contract, I received a bonus for taking us to the NCAA tournament, and that bonus was used to help pay the fine. I regret what happened, but it happened, and I will live with it.

## CHAPTER NINE

# My Coaching Pals

Throughout my life, I have been blessed to be associated with many great coaches, some for whom I played, some under whom I worked, and others against whom I coached. Gub McDonald was my baseball coach in sixth grade, and as I recall, he may have been the best coach I ever had other than Tex Winter. The organization was called Larned Recreation, and we gathered there with Gub two hours each morning.

But in terms of friends in the profession, Jud Heathcote—the legendary former coach at Michigan State—is my closest. How Jud and I met is actually kind of funny. I was Eddie Sutton's assistant at Arkansas, and I interviewed for the head coaching vacancy at Idaho State. I briefly accepted an offer to coach there, then changed my mind and returned to Arkansas to be with Eddie and a great bunch of players who were returning for the 1977-78 season, our Final Four year.

Soon after turning that job down, I attended a basketball camp in Georgia, and Jud was there. A group of coaches gathered to socialize one evening, and I was engaged in conversation when I heard this big voice yell from across the room, "Hey, Keady, you may never get another chance to be a head coach." I turned, and it was Jud. I really didn't know him well, but I knew who he was. We visited, and our friendship developed quickly and easily. Jud and I are a lot alike. Sometimes we are blunt. Sometimes we will tell you something you may not want to hear. But always we are honest above everything else.

Many people have asked why the Purdue and Michigan State coaching staffs are so close. Certainly, it is a relationship Jud and I nurtured. There was a time when Jud—and later Tom Izzo when Tom replaced Jud at Michigan State—used our program as a model in their attempt to get their kids to play harder. Jud admired that quality in our teams, and so did Tom. On the court, we had some great battles. Often Jud would bring his team into Mackey Arena and beat us, and we would turn around and go into old Jennison Fieldhouse or into the Breslin Center and beat them. Each team usually played well on the road in this rivalry, and that's something you don't often see in college basketball, or in any athletic endeavor for that matter. Some of my fondest coaching memories involve games against Jud, or later against Tom.

To explain how close Jud and I are, I allowed myself to visit with Jud in his office after our games in East Lansing. That's something most coaches don't traditionally do after games, but sometimes I would storm into Jud's office and vent about how poor the officiating was. If you can believe this, Jud often agreed with me, even after they had beaten us. Again, that tells you something about how honest Jud is.

I always admired the way Jud coached his guards, and he developed some of the best in Magic Johnson, Scott Skiles, Steve Smith, and Shawn Respert, just to name a few. When Jud's guards played the way they were capable of playing, Michigan State was extremely difficult to beat. We stress man-to-man defense at Purdue, and when we played Michigan State, our defense had to be at its best.

One of my favorite on-the-road stories also is one of Jud's favorites. We were in East Lansing preparing to play the Spartans and were in the middle of an intense practice in old Jennison. You have to understand that before they built the Breslin Center, many Michigan State teams shared practice time in the fieldhouse. As we were practicing, the Michigan State fencing team was gathering for its daily practice and was at one end of the facility. The late Dr. Bill Combs, who was a great, tough guy, was our team physician and was on the trip to Michigan State. The fencing team coach approached Dr. Combs and told him that our coaching staff and team would have to leave the premises so that his team could conduct its practice in private. To which Bill responded, "See Coach Keady standing over there. Well, if I tell him what you just told me, he probably will come over here, remove that sword from your hands and stick it right up your ass! I would suggest that you and your team keep its distance from Coach Keady and his players." Well after that, the fencing coach and his team were suddenly more than willing to share space with us.

Part of what makes coaching so enjoyable is the relationships a coach develops and nurtures with other coaches.

Without a doubt, Jud always will have a special place in my heart. Right there with Jud is Bruce Weber, my long-time assistant, first at Western Kentucky and then at Purdue. I could not be happier for Bruce and his team with all that they accomplished at Illinois during the 2004-05 season, coming within a possession or two of beating North Carolina in the NCAA tournament championship game.

Bruce's hiring at Western Kentucky is a story in and of itself. Bruce, who was living in Milwaukee, sought and was granted an interview for an assistant's job. He traveled to Bowling Green, Kentucky, to interview with me, and I wasn't there. We had gotten confused about the dates. Bruce ended up speaking to my assistant coaches at the time, Clem Haskins and Ray Hite. They spoke highly of him, so I phoned Bruce to arrange another interview. However, Bruce said that unfortunately, he didn't have the money to drive back down. So I interviewed him over the phone, and after a great talk, I hired him on the spot.

When I got the Purdue job in April, 1980, Bruce joined me in West Lafayette. Over the years, Bruce was a terrific jack-of-all trades. He could "X and O" with the best of them, recruit, plan trips, run our camps, and make great in-game strategy modifications. I don't know how many times we won games based on an idea Bruce had. And he was a great teacher during our practices.

For a time in the 1990s, I was concerned that no one would hire Bruce as a head coach. He would interview and then finish second to someone else. But in 1998, he finally got the break he needed and was on his way to Southern Illinois in Carbondale. SIU had struggled for several years, but Bruce, along with help from Matt Painter, did a tremendous job

My friendship with Bruce Weber goes all the way back to my days at Western Kentucky. I'm happy that all the hard work he put in for me at Purdue was finally rewarded with a Big Ten head coaching position at Illinois.

*Purdue Sports Information*

there. When Bill Self left for Kansas, Illinois gave Bruce the chance of a lifetime to coach in the Big Ten. All the hard work he put in at Purdue and then at Southern Illinois was finally rewarded.

Of course, two coaches who are associated with Purdue—Ward "Piggy" Lambert and John Wooden—also are among my favorites. Piggy was an idol of mine when I was young, because Sam Butterfield, who hired me at Hutchinson Junior College, talked about Piggy all the time. In the off-season, Sam and I would travel to Montana and do hail-damage adjustments for an insurance company. On those trips, Sam would tell me what a great coach Lambert was. Isn't it interesting that in 1998, I broke Lambert's record for career victories at Purdue?

Lambert's best player probably was Wooden, who is a very special man to me. Throughout my coaching career, I used a lot of Coach Wooden's practice drills. I attended many coaching clinics that featured Wooden. He was at a Fellowship of Christian Athletes camp in Estes Park, Colorado, one time, and at that camp he gave me a play to run during a last-second-shot situation. That play won some games for me over the years. Then, for us to take part in the John Wooden Tradition each year in Indianapolis was special for our players and for our basketball program.

I think another reason I am so fond of Wooden is because he and I had similar backgrounds. Each of us came up the hard way. When he was a boy, his family lived on a farm near Martinsville, Indiana, and his dad ended up losing that farm. Coach Wooden's dad took a job as a masseur in an artesian spa in Martinsville, and it was at that point in Wooden's life that he became involved in basketball, leading his team to

**Legendary coach John Wooden and I have many things in common, from our family backgrounds to our love of Purdue University.** *Purdue Sports Information*

Indiana's high school state finals three times before coming to school at Purdue.

The similarities don't end there. I always enjoyed being an educator, and so did Coach Wooden, who was a high school English teacher and basketball coach in South Bend long before he coached all those great teams at UCLA. To this day, Coach Wooden is a great teacher, and I hope I still am, too. When we grew up, education was everything. The mindset was to earn a degree, advance yourself, and live a better lifestyle than the past generation. The only striking difference between us is that John Wooden coached 10 National Championship teams, and I didn't coach one.

## CHAPTER TEN

# The Era of the Big Dog

The early 1990s were exciting times for our basketball program, in part because we were successfully recruiting the player—Glenn Robinson—whom almost everyone in the nation was after. At six-foot-eight, Glenn had the ability to dominate a game on the interior, or pull his man away from the basket and spot up for a three-pointer. Obviously, our staff made many trips to Roosevelt High School in Gary, Indiana, to watch the player who went by the nickname "Big Dog." We started recruiting Glenn when he was in junior high school. We could see that this kid was going to be special, the kind of player who could make a significant difference in our program's success. Glenn led Gary Roosevelt to Indiana's 1991 high school state championship, defeating Indianapolis Brebeuf and Alan Henderson in the title game. Henderson went on to star at Indiana University and then in the NBA.

We had an "in" with him because his high school coach, Ron Heflin, was a fan of Purdue and liked our staff. Our proximity also benefited Glenn, because it is only 90 miles from his home in Gary to West Lafayette. That would enable his family to attend almost every game. As we recruited Glenn, he bonded well with all of our coaches. Glenn and my former assistant Frank Kendrick were close, and Frank was a personable man who had a good relationship with all of our players.

While we felt we were in good shape with Glenn throughout the recruiting process, I learned years later that he came close to changing his mind and selecting UNLV. At that time, however, I didn't know that Glenn was considering UNLV. UNLV coach Jerry Tarkanian was in Gary trying to sway Glenn late in the recruiting process. Luckily, Tarkanian's effort was too little, too late. He wasn't going to pry Glenn away from us.

We were thrilled when Glenn made it official that he would become a Boilermaker in 1991. Considering the amount of money that is out there today for great high school players or kids with one year of college experience, if Glenn would have graduated several years later, he probably would have gone directly from high school into the NBA draft. But we were thankfully living in a different basketball era then. At that time, exceptional young players frequently opted for at least two or three years of college basketball. Glenn stayed at Purdue three years, although he was not academically eligible to participate in 1991-92, his freshman season.

**A good deal of our attention during the 1990-91 season was spent on a player who wasn't even a Purdue Boilermaker—yet. Our recruitment of Glenn Robinson, "The Big Dog," was an achievement many years in the making.**
*Purdue Sports Information*

Certainly, we spent a lot of time during the 1990-91 season recruiting Glenn and following his progress, but we also had a good team of our own to coach at Purdue. Jimmy Oliver, Chuckie White, and Dave Barrett were the senior members of a team that finished 17-12, losing to Temple in the opening round of the NCAA tournament's East Regional in College Park, Maryland.

With Jimmy Oliver, we had a player who really could shoot it, but was lacking confidence in himself. In fact, Jimmy was better than he thought he was.

Chuckie White had battled with a hamstring injury early in his career but played exceptionally well in 1990-91, leading the Big Ten Conference in rebounding.

That team would have been better than it was, but after the first semester, shooting guard Woody Austin was ruled academically ineligible, which took away a great deal of our perimeter offense. In my 11th season at Purdue, I experienced my first mid-season academic casualty. That team began 9-2, but without Woody's scoring punch we struggled in the Big Ten. We experienced a 1-7 stretch in late January and into February, but went 6-1 in our last seven regular-season games to earn an NCAA tournament berth.

As we were preparing to leave for College Park and the opening round of the tournament, the midwest was struck by an ice storm. The storm was so bad that a huge tree in our backyard broke and fell across our backporch. We left with this large tree resting right up against the back of our Lafayette home.

We got to College Park safely but then played poorly in an 80-63 loss to John Chaney's Temple team. Temple played an excellent zone defense and was a superb team. The season could have been a better one if we had not lost Woody to grades, but we had reason to smile late in the season when we knew for sure that Glenn Robinson was indeed a Boilermaker. The downside was that we learned Glenn would be a Proposition 48 casualty, which meant that he could not practice with us or play in games during the 1991-92 season.

Along with Glenn, we also recruited Cuonzo Martin out of East St. Louis, Illinois. Cuonzo, now a member of Matt Painter's Purdue coaching staff, came to us with damaged knees—so much so that athletic trainer Denny Miller told me that Cuonzo would never play basketball for us. Denny said, "It is bone on bone. He will never play."

But what a heart Cuonzo had. And what a great leader he was, too. It's interesting that in 1991-92, Glenn could not play because of academics, and Cuonzo's knees were a mess. But two years later, those two guys took us to within one victory of the Final Four.

✦ ✦ ✦ ✦

I knew that our 1991-92 season would be one of transition, and it was. Thank God that Woody Austin regained his eligibility and gave us the scorer we sorely needed. Ian Stanback, a young center-forward, played a lot of minutes during that season, and Linc Darner, who now coaches at Division II St. Joseph's College in Rensselaer, Indiana, started a lot of games at guard. Cuonzo—bad knees and all—started at forward, and Craig Riley was our senior post player. We tried to mix and match that team as best we could.

We got off to a 7-2 start, but we knew that we would have to play a lot of young kids, and when we got into the Big Ten schedule, there were going to be some rough moments.

Cuonzo Martin was a great leader who didn't allow a pair of damaged knees to ruin his collegiate career. Instead, he averaged 13.1 points per game over the course of his career, and transformed himself into a deadly three-point shooter.

*Doug Pensinger/Getty Images*

One of the highlights during the year was our final regular-season game against an Indiana team that was ranked No. 4 and would advance to the Final Four in Minneapolis. We beat them 61-59, and were invited to play in the postseason NIT. We hosted the first two rounds in Mackey Arena and defeated Butler (82-56) and Texas Christian (67-51). We needed one more victory to advance to New York City and the Final Four. Things appeared to be in our favor as we were scheduled to host Florida at Mackey Arena. But Mackey was not available because our women's team was hosting NCAA tournament games. So we moved the game from West Lafayette to Market Square Arena in Indianapolis, where Florida defeated us 74-67, capping an 18-15 season. It would have been great to take that team to New York, but we also knew that our days without Glenn Robinson now were over.

It didn't take long for Glenn to make an impact on the college game. We opened our 1992-93 season against 16th-ranked Connecticut in the Hall of Fame Tipoff Classic in Springfield, Massachusetts. Glenn led us to a 73-69 victory against one of Jim Calhoun's great UConn teams. While I'm not into handing out a lot of personal accolades, that game against UConn reminds me that I finished with a winning record against Calhoun, Bob Knight, and Denny Crum, each of whom is in the Hall of Fame category of coaching greats.

I realized after the UConn game what an unbelievable addition Glenn was to our program. He was a player who could score at will. We won our first nine games and were ranked ninth when No. 3 Michigan came to Mackey Arena for a game in early January. They beat us 80-70, and then we went to Minnesota and were beaten 81-60. We struggled in the Big Ten because our guard play never really came along as we hoped that winter. We really were disappointed when we lost to Northwestern (62-59) in Mackey Arena; the Wildcats ran all kinds of backdoor sets against us. Bruce Weber, who was my assistant then, told me recently that I threatened to fire him after that loss to Northwestern. Frankly, I was ready to fire everybody, including myself when we lost that game. We finished the Big Ten season 9-9 but were still ranked 22nd when we played Rhode Island in the opening round of the NCAA tournament in Winston-Salem, North Carolina.

Rhode Island had very good team that year and defeated us, 74-68. After that game, our local Lafayette newspaper, the *Journal and Courier*, surveyed its readership, asking if it was time for me to go elsewhere. I was extremely bothered by that. I had a lot of chances to leave Purdue—I could have gone to Arizona State and I could have gone to Texas—but that loyalty didn't mean anything to people. Fans demand instant success. The paper had an "800" call-in number, asking readers if Purdue should fire Keady. I said, "Wait a minute!" That Rhode Island team was the No. 8 seed, and we were the No. 9 seed. Rhode Island had a senior-dominated team, and we were relatively young. Matt Painter was our only senior that year.

✦ ✦ ✦ ✦

We made it through all the fallout from the newspaper's survey and rededicated ourselves to winning. The only concern in the spring of 1993 was whether Glenn might leave for the NBA. I didn't approach our discussions about his future with a focus on whether he would leave. Instead, I talked with Glenn about what he could do to improve his game and how much better prepared for the NBA he would be with an additional season of college basketball. Looking back now, our loss

**After Glenn Robinson's amazing season in 1992-93, I told Glenn what he needed to do to improve his game in the upcoming season and prepare himself for a long career in the NBA. He took my advice, choosing to return in 1993-94 for a spectacular season which saw him win the National Player of the Year award.**
*Purdue Sports Information*

to Rhode Island may have helped in Glenn's decision to stay at Purdue for another year. Had we enjoyed a long run in the 1993 NCAA tournament, Glenn might have entered the 1993 NBA draft.

Over the spring, summer, and early fall, everyone worked hard and concentrated on their conditioning. All the kids had good attitudes, and we benefited from the dedication of role players Kenny Williams, Cornelius McNary, and Linc

Darner, who were all big practice guys. They gave Robinson, Stanback, and Brandon Brantley excellent competition each day in practice. As we prepared to open the 1993-94 season, I knew this team's character was exceptional.

With the exception of the 1987-88 team, when Troy Lewis, Todd Mitchell, and Everette Stephens were seniors, the 1993-94 team quickly became the best offensive team we've ever had. In addition to Glenn being a year older and having a season of college experience under his belt, Cuonzo developed into a terrific three-point shooter. During Cuonzo's freshman and sophomore seasons, he was a combined 0-for-7 from three-point range. As a junior in 1993-94, Cuonzo went 88 of 196 from beyond the arc and averaged 16.3 points to complement Glenn, who averaged 30.3 points and 10.1 rebounds. I told Cuonzo during the summer of 1993 that he needed to develop that three-point shot so that we could take some of the pressure off of our interior players. Together with Darner and guard Matt Waddell, Cuonzo opened things up on the inside by hitting outside shots. He used his cleverness to move without the ball within our passing game and get open looks.

We were ranked 21st in the 1993-94 preseason poll and began the year in the Great Alaska Shootout. We defeated Wisconsin-Green Bay (74-69), Weber State (97-78), and Portland (88-73) to win the Great Alaska Shootout. Glenn played extremely well in Anchorage, and as we returned to Indiana, I knew that we were set up for an excellent season. However, I did not know at that time that we had a team that would earn the No. 1 seed in the NCAA tournament's Southeast Regional.

We won our first 14 games, climbing to No. 9 in the polls before a six-point loss at Wisconsin in January knocked us back to 12th. We turned right around from that loss and beat No. 8 Indiana at home in overtime, 83-76. Then we went on to win our first Big Ten championship since 1988 by posting a 14-4 conference mark. Certainly, Glenn and Cuonzo had excellent seasons, but our role players were very special that season as well. Stanback made lots of big plays. He would get a steal if we needed it when the game was close. Or he could take the opponent's post man and really defend him. I liked to call Ian our secret weapon because he could do a lot of things and do those things during important parts of the game. Guards Porter Roberts and Todd Foster were young members of that team, but each made huge contributions during the season. Justin Jennings was a young forward who was an extremely good athlete. Together, those guys—plus Herb Dove—were damn good players. And center Brandon Brantley played real well for a young kid. He had 15 rebounds in one game.

We had all of the pieces, but the biggest piece of all, of course, was Glenn. Down the stretch it was evident how much Glenn had improved that season. He developed a great shooting touch and was a great competitor. He had those long arms, and defenders just could not stop him. His post moves were incredibly tough to defend, especially what I like to call the cross-over or draw-through. We worked on that every day in practice with all of our big guys, but for Glenn it just came natural. Really, he didn't even need to be coached on it. But when Glenn did need instruction, he was a good listener. He was very easy to coach.

We lost twice in January and twice in February, but we got hot at just the right time. Late in the season, it seemed like Glenn was unstoppable. We won our final five regular-season games, including a great 95-94 victory at third-ranked Michigan on March 6. We moved from ninth to sixth in the polls after that victory, and when we ended the regular season with an 87-77 victory against Illinois a week later, the voters pushed us up to No. 3, which gave us a No. 1 seed in the NCAA tournament.

We began our NCAA tournament run in Lexington, Kentucky, at Rupp Arena, where we defeated Central Florida (98-67) and Alabama (83-73). The Alabama victory was especially rewarding because they were a very good team. Until then we had rarely beaten Southeastern Conference teams. We struggled with Florida, LSU, and Auburn in the NCAA tournament. Those SEC schools always featured great athletes. The coaching staff did not mention it to the players, but we were very concerned about playing Alabama.

Then we moved on to the Sweet Sixteen at Knoxville, Tennessee, and defeated 13th-ranked Kansas, 83-78. Our team was within a victory of advancing to the Final Four for the first time in 14 years, but we had a problem that no one was aware of outside of our team. With eight minutes remaining in our victory against Kansas, one of their post players fell on Glenn, who sustained a back injury. At the time of the contact, it did not bother Glenn, because he was warmed up and in the flow of a game and loose. But when Glenn got out of bed the next morning, his back was killing him. If we could have faced off against Duke just one day later, he would have been okay. But we played Thursday and Saturday, and he was hurting on Saturday for our matchup with the No. 6 Blue Devils.

We didn't say much about Glenn's back, and our training staff attempted to get him ready to play. He started the Duke game off pretty well, but in the end, Glenn's back injury was a huge factor in a 69-60 loss to a Duke team that was led by Grant Hill. Their forwards played very well against Glenn, who was less than 100 percent. Considering Glenn's injury, I had serious doubts about whether we could beat Duke. I hoped that someone would step up and take the star's place. But Duke beat us up pretty well, and their defense really got to us. Cuonzo and Waddell played well, but it wasn't enough.

I also remember that a call went against Duke, and during the next timeout, Duke coach Mike Krzyzewski got all over the referees, which seemed to turn the game. We finished the season 29-5, but a loss like that one—when there was a Final Four berth on the line—really hurt. It definitely crossed my mind that I might never have that opportunity again. I also was frustrated with the refereeing. There were some strange calls in that game. They called us for stepping across the end line on an inbounds play, and they whistled us for a couple of three-second violations that didn't agree with me. To make matters worse, I heard from some of our fans that Grant Hill's father was in a restaurant eating dinner with the officials after the game. That was just talk, but it didn't make me feel any better to hear it in the days following that loss.

Just when I thought that things couldn't get any worse, they did. We flew back to West Lafayette, and as I got off the plane, I was carrying several of Pat's bags and slipped and fell onto her, knocking her to the ground. Pat hit her head on the pavement, and for a moment, I thought I had killed her. Obviously, that was not a fun trip home. From that day on, Pat has always walked behind me when we get off a plane. Not only did I feel bad about the damn Duke game, but I almost killed my wife. I thought, "What the hell is going on here?" It must have been bad-luck week.

Within the next several weeks, it became evident that Glenn was going to make himself available for the 1994 NBA draft. He and I really hadn't talked about whether or not he would return for his senior year, but I knew in my heart that he was going to go pro. Once it was decided, a press conference was scheduled in Glenn's hometown of Gary. I was happy for Glenn, and happy for us, because we had a lot to do with Glenn being selected National Player of the Year in 1994.

Pat and I made sure Glenn wore a tuxedo for the John Wooden Award presentation in California. We wanted to be certain that everything was first class for Glenn, who really was a good kid. A lot of that was because Pat helped Glenn with his social graces. It wasn't that Glenn did anything poorly, but Pat helped him step up in those areas. Glenn trusted Pat and accepted her advice.

I really liked Glenn's mother and stepfather, who always were very appreciative of what we had done for Glenn. But I did not like Glenn's agent, who acted sneaky. What the hell, I knew Glenn was going to go pro. I wanted him to sign with Eugene Parker, who is a Fort Wayne-based agent and a Purdue grad who has many NFL stars as clients. And I wanted Glenn to sign with Nike, but he did not want Nike. I think Glenn thought we wanted him to be like Michael Jordan, but we just wanted him to be Glenn Robinson. I wanted Glenn to be his own man. While Glenn did not seek a lot of advice from me, he did not hide from me, either. He would come into my office and talk, and he was always was up front with me.

Of course I couldn't help but think what a special team we would have had in 1994-95 had Glenn come back for his senior season. But 1994 was our chance to get a national championship. In June of 1994, the Milwaukee Bucks used their first-round draft pick—the top overall selection—to select Glenn, who went on to have an excellent career, primarily in Milwaukee. In June 2005, Glenn experienced the joy of a championship, helping the San Antonio Spurs win another title.

## CHAPTER ELEVEN

# Two More Titles

When a star player like Glenn Robinson leaves a college program, the natural reaction is to center on the negative—that the team will be unable to sustain the momentum and confidence that it acquired during the seasons that the star player was there. Fortunately, Glenn's supporting cast enjoyed winning and knew how to meet the challenge of playing without someone who averaged 30 points a game in 1993-94. Our 1994-95 and 1995-96 teams also were Big Ten Conference champions, placing us in some very exclusive company. We became the first Big Ten team since the great Ohio State clubs of 1960, '61, and '62 to win three consecutive conference titles.

For me, the most rewarding thing about those three conference championship teams is that each had its own strength and personality. Obviously, Glenn was the focal point of the 1994 Big Ten champions. But the 1995 team (25-7) and the 1996 team (26-6) each had a unique identity as well. The 1994-95 team was a smart group of overachievers—a team that was all about heart. The 1995-96 team was a great defensive team.

There were concerns during the summer of 1994, because two of our three senior captains—small forward Cuonzo Martin and guard Matt Waddell—underwent knee surgery. Cuonzo was our No. 2 scorer behind Glenn in 1994, and Matt was an extremely smart guard who could run our offense or sink an important shot. As those thoughts loomed large, we began the season with a pair of exhibition wins before heading to the Big Island Invitational in Hilo, Hawaii, for our non-conference opener. We played three games in three days in extremely humid conditions after a lengthy flight from the mainland. All of us wondered if Cuonzo and Matt would be able to play extended minutes without pain. In fact, I really didn't think Zo or Matt would play. Much to my delight, not only did each play, but they played great. We defeated Niagra (71-60) in the opening round and then beat New Orleans (84-71) in the semifinals. The championship game was a terrific contest, one that had an NCAA-tournament like feel to it. We beat Iowa State, which was coached by Tim Floyd, 88-87 in overtime.

I think an unknown key to that championship in Hilo was our third captain, Tim Ervin, a walk-on who did not play a lot. Tim was a great leader, maybe one of the best that we had in my 25 years at Purdue. He had a wonderful ability to keep

**Sometimes it's the players who don't see much game action who provide a big boost to the team. That was the case with walk-on Tim Ervin in 1994-95.**

*Purdue Sports Information*

all the kids focused, making sure they were doing things together on weekends or on road trips. That team might have a pizza party, and Tim would help organize it. He was an extremely positive person who was a vocal guy when the team huddled. He got everybody jacked up at just the right time.

In addition to Tim, that 1994-95 team benefitted from the addition of two talented freshmen: Brad Miller, who now plays for the NBA's Sacramento Kings, and Chad Austin, a great shooter who has done well playing professional basketball in Europe. We also had added forward Roy Hairston, who was the 1994 junior college player of the year. All those guys performed well in Hawaii, which left everyone feeling good about the team.

But in athletics, fortunes turn quickly. Almost as fast as we started 3-0, we fell to 3-3. We flew directly from Hawaii to Detroit for an appearance in the Great Eight, a made-for-TV two-night event at The Palace in Auburn Hills, Michigan. We played Missouri, and it was evident from the early moments of the game that our legs were gone. We couldn't get lift on our shots, and we just couldn't play defense like usual. Missouri beat us 69-66. The six-game, season-opening road trip continued with a trip to James Madison in Harrisonburg, Virginia. Their crowd was into it, and they beat us 91-87. From there we had a game at Western Michigan, and again we did not defend as well as we were capable of doing. Western Michigan defeated us 90-81.

Obviously, that was unwise scheduling on my part. In those days, I was doing all of our non-conference scheduling. But we recovered from a trip that took us from West Lafayette to Hawaii to Detroit to Virginia to Kalamazoo and back to West Lafayette. We got our legs back under us and then won six in a row and 13 of 15. Everyone started playing better, and Cuonzo and Matt really started playing well.

Eventually, Roy Hairston began to help us the way we envisioned him contributing when we recruited him. For about half of that season, Roy was a pain in the butt. Then he went through the most impressive attitude turnaround of any player I have ever coached. He literally did a 180-degree turn. At one point in 1995, he wanted to leave Purdue. He felt that we were not utilizing his talent in the way that he anticipated. By his senior year in 1996, he had done such a 180 that we couldn't get rid of him—and we didn't want to. He had become so happy at Purdue that he wanted to be around our basketball family all of the time.

The beauty of the 1995 Big Ten championship, of which Roy was a key piece, is that after three league games, we were 1-2. We lost at Michigan, beat Minnesota in Mackey Arena, and then lost a tough game to Illinois in Mackey. Beginning with an 84-83 victory at Iowa, which was ranked 10th when we went to Iowa City, our 1995 team won 14 of its final 15 Big Ten games, which is one of the best stretches ever in Purdue basketball history. To achieve something like that, a coach must have great senior leadership, which we had from Cuonzo, Matt, and Timmy. But it takes more than just leadership, and we had some very good athletes on that team. The junior class featured skilled players like Roy Hairston, Brandon Brantley, Porter Roberts, Justin Jennings, Todd Foster, and Herb Dove. I also can't emphasize enough how much Brad Miller and Chad Austin—our freshmen—helped us that year. They were very good for a pair of freshmen.

We entered the 1995 NCAA tournament ranked 12th in the final polls and were placed in the Midwest Regional in

Austin, Texas. In the opening round, we played Wisconsin-Green Bay, which at that time was coached by Dick Bennett. Green Bay played exceptionally well, and quite frankly, we were fortunate to escape with a 49-48 victory. Late in that game, there was a collision involving Cuonzo, and the official called a blocking foul on Green Bay. He just as easily could have called a charge on Zo. Had the call gone the other way, we probably would have lost that game. That call really helped us, which reminded me that maybe things were evening out after the bad calls we received in the one-point, 1990 NCAA tournament loss to Texas, on whose court we now played against Green Bay.

In the second round, we played an extremely talented Memphis team, and ended up losing, 75-73. Again, I was frustrated, because Big Ten official Tom Rucker refereed that game, and I did not think he did a good job representing our conference. But that's just me. At the end of that game, Memphis missed a shot, and as Roy Hairston attempted to go for the rebound, one of the Memphis players grabbed Roy's jersey, held him, and tore his jersey as one of their guys gathered an offensive rebound and scored the game-winning basket. I could have gone off after that loss, but I didn't. I really started getting better with my sportsmanship. My wife, Pat, had reminded me that it was time to be a better sportsman.

✦ ✦ ✦ ✦

While we lost three excellent leaders from the 1995 Big Ten championship club, many underestimated what we had coming back in 1996. First of all, those guys were excellent defensive players, and we had Todd Foster, who was a tremendous competitor. At every practice, Todd was like one of those little devils in a whirlwind. Todd made everyone practice harder. He was a farm kid from Illinois who was an excellent small-school football and basketball player in high school. Sometimes he played like a football guy during our practices, which wasn't all bad. Justin Jennings was a very athletic forward who would come off the bench and get dunks for us, firing up his teammates and the crowd in the process. Porter Roberts was our point guard and was one of those players who could go all night. Porter had a motor that just never ran out of power. Roy Hairston continued his development into a really good all-around player. We gained additional toughness from Herb Dove, and Brandon Brantley was a very good rebounder. All of those players complemented each other well. While the core group was comprised of seniors, Chad Austin and Brad Miller now were sophomores and provided a lot of scoring.

We were unranked throughout most of the non-conference season after losing our season opener. We were ranked 24th in the first poll, but we lost our opener to the same team that had booted us from the NCAA tournament in the year prior. 12th-ranked Memphis defeated us by 15 points in a game played in Kansas City, but then we quickly recovered to win our next four. Then in early December, we lost by 17 to No. 2 Villanova in the John Wooden Classic in a game played at The Pond in Anaheim, California. In our high-profile non-conference games, we did not perform as well as we could, so it's easy to understand why a lot of people overlooked us. In fact, I apologized to Mr. Wooden—a proud Purdue graduate—in the press conference after the Villanova game. I told him that we played so poorly that we didn't deserve to be invited back to an event named in his honor.

When Big Ten play began, I did not think that this team was on the verge of a third consecutive Big Ten title despite a 10-2 record. But credit this team—they figured out a way to win, and without Cuonzo Martin, I was afraid that they couldn't. Todd kind of took Zo's place as leader. Our special season on the court was balanced out by a troubling season off the court for my family. Our daughter, Lisa, who passed away in June 2005, was injured in a fall in her New Jersey home the day of our January 10 game at Northwestern. Then, later that same week, my father, Lloyd, passed away in California.

When Lisa was injured, we really didn't know what was going on. Pat's dear friend, Marilyn Meadors, was with Pat at the Northwestern game in Evanston, Illinois. We got a call before the game, informing us that Lisa was in surgery in a Hackensack, New Jersey hospital. Pat went right from the arena to Chicago's O'Hare Airport and flew to New Jersey. We defeated Northwestern, but I did not know until we got back to Lafayette that night what was going on with my daughter. When Pat arrived at the hospital, she really didn't know what was going on, either. Lisa had hit her head on the edge of a glass table and was in a coma for 17 days. It was a long, emotional time for us, and I traveled to see her every weekend. We were scheduled to play at Minnesota on January 13, and I got the news on Friday that my father had passed away. I flew to California for the funeral, which was hard for me, because my father is the best man I have ever known in my life.

What was so heart-warming for me is that our players took those two difficult events and protected me. They went to war and took it out on the guys they were playing. I was flying all over the country that week, but I arrived in Minneapolis in time to coach the game, which was played on

Saturday afternoon. Bruce Weber and my other assistants—Frank Kendrick and Jay Price—did a great job preparing the team on Friday night.

On Saturday, we beat Minnesota 76-62 in Williams Arena. It's the only time in my coaching career I ever cried after a game. Reporters asked me about my father, and I broke down. He was a wonderful man. I was thrilled that we won, but I also was exhausted. I had been in New Jersey, Sacramento, and then Minnesota. It was tough, but Pat really helped me through that time. She kept me informed, and she kept telling me, "Everything will be okay." I've always trusted Pat, who is an extremely wonderful and strong woman. Marilyn Meadors also was a great help to Pat, being at Pat's side every second.

With everything going on that week, I considered not coaching the game at Minnesota. Then, everyone—my players and coaches—said they wanted me there in Minneapolis. Pat told me it was okay. After Lisa's surgery, there wasn't anything I could do. However, I learned that it is important to talk to people in a coma. They can hear what you are saying to them. When the person wakes up, they often say they remember something that was said to them. It is amazing to me how that works. We asked the doctors when they thought Lisa would wake up, but the doctors would not commit to a timetable. We asked the nurses, and the nurses said, "She will wake up in about 15 days." The center in which Lisa stayed in specialized in dealing with those types of injuries.

After that week—victories at Northwestern and Minnesota during stressful times—there wasn't any doubt that this team could win a third consecutive Big Ten championship. At that point, we thought we had our foot in the door.

Beginning with that victory at Northwestern, we won 14 of our final 17 Big Ten games to finish 15-3 in the league. We climbed to No. 4 in the final poll and earned the No. 1 seed in the West Regional. That No. 1 seed is one of the most gratifying experiences I've had in coaching, because we really did not deserve that blessing. But because that group had played so well as a team, it was rewarded with a top seed.

We were playing so well late in the year that the Duke coaches called our office and wanted to know what the hell we were doing defensively. I thought, "Duke is calling us?" Those kids were coachable, and they used their defensive drills to ultimate success. Roy Hairston was a guy who really bought into playing defense. He was happy, and he became an excellent student. When I went to watch Roy when he played junior college basketball for Hutchinson, Kansas, I attended a Thanksgiving tournament in Garden City, Kansas. The night I saw him play, he had seven steals. But their coaches kept telling me that Roy was a great three-point shooter. He really was not a great three-point shooter, but he was a great defensive player—and that's what I wanted Roy to be. Had he been a great three-point shooter, that would have been a plus. But that's not why I recruited him.

What a change that was to see Roy's adjustment. When he was a junior, we beat Indiana, and when I went into our locker room, he was moping around. I went berserk. I went off on Roy about being selfish. I told him, "We just beat Indiana, and you should be happy." But he was a New Jersey kid who didn't know what the Purdue-Indiana series was all about. However, by the end of the 1996 regular season, Roy understood what we needed from him.

**Roy Hairston became a key contributor during our run to the 1995 and 1996 Big Ten championships. He turned his attitude around and bought into playing defense to become the player I envisioned when I recruited him from my old stomping grounds at Hutchinson Junior College in Kansas.**

*Purdue Sports Information*

I thought we might make some noise in that 1996 NCAA tournament, but I guess our attitudes weren't cut into what we needed from them. We played the No. 16 seed, Western Carolina, in the opening round in The Pit in Albuquerque, New Mexico, and almost became the first No. 1 seed to lose to a No. 16. We hung on for a 73-71 victory, but Western Carolina missed a last-second three-pointer to win it. The day after that game, we began to prepare for a second-round game with Georgia, and I was not happy. I came into the hotel lobby, and our players did not appear to be focused on the task at hand. I went off on them. I told them, "Georgia is a great team that is coached by Tubby Smith, who is a great coach. You guys don't know anything about him, and he has a group of seniors who were ranked the No. 1 recruiting class in the nation when they came to Georgia."

After that our guys wanted to know, "Why is Coach Keady so upset?" They were not ready to play that game, and it showed. After we lost 76-69, Porter Roberts said he was glad it was over, because he was ready for the NBA. Our guys just did not have their heads screwed on correctly after we won the Big Ten championship. Having received the No. 1 seed, I don't think our players were realistic about what was happening to them. We were lucky to get that seed, but it only gives an opponent a greater desire to knock you off. That experience was an interesting scenario and gave me the opportunity to study people's attitudes. My players' attitudes had been wonderful during the regular season, but they did not understand that at the NCAA level, a team must start over. It is a new season once the tournament begins. They probably had gotten to the point where they thought they were a little better than they really were.

After the Georgia game, a television reporter said to me, "One of your players [Brad Miller] said that if this team had run a little more, it could have won." I went berserk. I told the reporter that the interview was over, and I stormed out. That is the only time in my life that I walked out of a press conference before it was scheduled to end. I was in a poor mood, and to make matters worse, as I got onto our team bus, someone was outside the bus protesting something, and I wanted to get off the bus and confront the man. Pat grabbed me and said, "Sit down!"

Then I got up and said to the team, "Who in the hell said in the media room that if we would fastbreak more, we could have won?" Brad Miller would never lie, and he said, "That was me, Coach." I said, "You dumb SOB … shut up!" Brad started crying. I did not know that Brad's answer had been taken out of context. I later found out that Brad was talking about what the team might do in 1996-97. That's just me. I have a short fuse, and I was upset anyway because we had lost to Georgia. But I love Brad Miller for his honesty. He is a guy who has remained close to our program. In fact, during my final few seasons at Purdue, Brad came back to campus to visit more than any of our former players, which meant so much to me. He was a key piece in two of those three consecutive Big Ten titles.

Despite how the 1996 season ended, it still amazes me that we won three consecutive Big Ten championships and 80 of 98 games in doing so. As a collective, we worked our tails off, we put in long hours, and we recruited. I also wondered, "Is the league no good?" That's because every time Purdue won a Big Ten title, someone would say that we did so because the league was down. For some reason, people do not want Purdue

**Brad Miller was a unique big man because in addition to being a good rebounder and scorer, he was also an excellent passer. He finished his Purdue career with 257 assists, good for 22nd all time.** *Purdue Sports Information*

to win big. That's one of the things that kept me here for 25 years. I wanted to show people that we did deserve to win big.

That streak of titles was also gratifying, because with the exception of Glenn Robinson and Brad Miller, we won them without NBA-caliber players. When Ohio State won three in a row in the early 1960s, they were like NBA All-Star teams with Jerry Lucas, John Havlicek, and Larry Siegfried. Every year that I coached at Purdue was special, but three consecutive Big Ten championships is a scenario I could hardly believe came true. Among the three, the 1996 Big Ten championship surprised me the most, but as I look back on that team, those guys all were basketball junkies. Brandon Brantley is still playing pro ball overseas. Justin Jennings is a coach now. Porter Roberts played pro ball for several years. Roy Hairston still is playing pro ball abroad. And Todd Foster is an assistant coach at Purdue under Matt Painter. So each senior was totally committed to basketball in some fashion. That commitment made for a wonderful, fun run.

## CHAPTER TWELVE

# A Redbird Joins the Crew

Throughout my 25 seasons at Purdue, we were fortunate to have many crowd-pleasing players, but power forward Brian Cardinal, who assistant coach Frank Kendrick nicknamed "Redbird," may have been the most popular. After redshirting during the 1995-96 season, Cardinal quickly made his presence felt as a redshirt freshman in 1996-97. Actually, Brian helped our 1995-96 team tremendously as a practice player.

Brian played basketball at Unity High School in Tolono, Illinois, just a short drive from the University of Illinois campus. He is the son of Rod Cardinal, who for years was the men's basketball team's athletic trainer at the University of Illinois. Today, Rod is the Fighting Illini's director of basketball operations for head coach Bruce Weber, my long-time Purdue assistant. Brian desperately wanted to play for Illinois coach Lou Henson, but Lou wasn't convinced that Brian could play at Illinois, and because Brian is Rod's son, I think Lou was in a difficult position. We wanted Brian at Purdue, and Penn State was recruiting him as well. But we were successful in convincing Brian that he would be a perfect Boilermaker.

With Chad Austin and Brad Miller entering their junior seasons in 1996-97, and with the addition of Cardinal, who now plays for the NBA's Memphis Grizzlies, we thought we had the makings of a solid team. We also had a talented group of freshmen—small forward Mike Robinson, shooting guard Jaraan Cornell, power forward Gary McQuay, and point guard Mosi Barnes. But this season began with more trouble than success. We were 4-2 after losses to Bowling Green and No. 6 Kentucky as we headed into first-semester final examinations week. At that time, we learned that Mike Robinson and Gary McQuay—who thought they were hotshots—had been arrested at a West Lafayette book store and charged with the left of several CDs. I suspended them for a game—our matchup with No. 22 Louisville in Indianapolis—and they were ordered to perform community service. They also were punished within our basketball family. They learned from their mistake, but I was extremely angry that they had chosen to do something so foolish that went against everything our basketball program stood for. It was hard for me, because I could not understand why our kids would not act in a classy manner. I wondered why they would get involved in an incident like that. I told them, "You are basketball players, but you are nothing special. You should act special, but you should not think that people should treat you differently."

When I arrived at the Tippecanoe County jail, the judges were gathered in Chicago for a convention, so there was only one judge in town who could decide what to do with them. As I entered the jail, I was fuming. Then the judge arrived and said to me, "I can see you will handle this okay, so I'm going to Chicago." The judge turned them over to my custody, because he could see that I was pissed off.

I met with Gary and Mike and told them that they had embarrassed a lot of people. I told them that we had spent 17 years building a program that is nationally respected, and that I was very disappointed that I could recruit two players who would think that they could go into a place of business and steal. I told them that as far as I was concerned, I would like to get rid of them, and that I would help them transfer. But they came to me one at a time and said that they wanted to make it right with me. They knew they were wrong. But they both had pretty good parents, and each chose to make a very big adjustment instead of transfer.

I could have given them a longer suspension, but I thought that basketball was their way of getting their lives in order. It was a difficult decision, and I almost kicked them off the team. Instead, we decided to see if we could save them. Nobody cares more about his players than I do. I didn't think any other coach could help them more than I could, so we kept them at Purdue. I was going to make them learn to do things correctly.

With Robinson and McQuay on the bench, Louisville beat us 88-72. After an easy win in our next game, we went on a two-game road trip to Oklahoma and Texas Christian that had me wondering if this was going to be one of those lost seasons. Oklahoma mauled us 82-58 in Norman, and TCU scored at will in pounding us 97-69 in Fort Worth, Texas. We couldn't do anything right. We could not guard, and we could not score. In each game, the other team took it to us. But Oklahoma and TCU had really good players, too.

On the way back from Texas Christian, Cardinal did something that showed me what a special player and leader he was. Brian got up from his seat on the plane and walked to where I was sitting. He handed me a two-page letter in which he expressed how sorry he was about the way the team had played against Oklahoma and TCU. In his letter, he wrote about how his dream always was to play in the Final Four, and this was what he would do to make things right with me. It was a long letter. I could see that this kid was a little bit different. Brian probably wanted to go to the Final Four more than any kid we ever had at Purdue. That letter was a testament to his commitment to Purdue basketball.

We were 5-5 when went to 24th-ranked Illinois for the opening game of the Big Ten season. We won that game 75-69 and turned the season around. It was the first of nine consecutive victories against Illinois for Cardinal and Peoria, Illinois, native Robinson. After everything that had happened to us in the previous month, the victory at Illinois gave us a chance to find confidence in each other. We managed a 12-6 conference record, which was good enough for another trip to the NCAA tournament, despite a 17-11 overall record.

We played first- and second-round games in the Southeast Regional in Memphis. In the opening round, we played Rhode Island, a team that had eliminated us from the 1993 NCAA tournament. This time, we trailed Rhode Island by three points in the closing seconds when Cardinal stepped beyond the three-point line and forced overtime after making

Brian Cardinal's impact on our basketball teams went far beyond the 1,584 points and 749 rebounds he collected in his Purdue career. His leadership both on and off the court was instrumental to our success. *Craig Jones/Getty Images*

a huge shot. Brad Miller had a 30-point game, and we beat Rhode Island 83-76 in overtime.

That gave us a second-round opportunity to play No. 1-ranked Kansas, which had an excellent team. We played well for 35 minutes, but in the end, they simply wore us down and won 75-61. Considering where this team was—both on and off the court—when we went to Illinois in early January, we completed a nice turnaround during that season. The thing I liked the most was that I saw the attitudes of several players begin to change for the better as the season progressed. This was a relatively young team that was forced to deal with a lot of adversity early in their careers, and they selected the proper path.

But they had a chance to win, and to win big. I guess I'm one of those guys who rarely is satisfied. I recall several times after seasons during which we would win a lot of games, I would go to the National Association of Basketball Coaches' meetings complaining about our team. It may have been after one of those mid-'90s seasons that Oklahoma coach Kelvin Sampson asked me, "How many games did you win, Keady?" I told Kelvin how many we had won, and Kelvin would say, "Shut up! We all would love to have that." I guess I took winning for granted in those days.

✦ ✦ ✦ ✦

I could sense that we had an opportunity to have an excellent 1997-98 season when Brad Miller, Chad Austin, and Brian Cardinal went to Australia in the summer of 1997 to participate in an international competition. We needed a point guard to go with a group that included Miller, Austin, Cardinal, and Jaraan Cornell. We had Alan Eldridge to run the

In the summer of 1997, (left to right) Chad Austin, Brian Cardinal, and Brad Miller had the opportunity to travel to Australia and represent America in international competition. *Purdue Sports Information*

point, and we also signed Tony Mayfield out of junior college in Tyler, Texas. Mike Robinson gave us an excellent player off the bench.

We began the season ranked No. 9 and prepared for a trip to the Great Alaska Shootout by winning games against Long Island, Valparaiso, and Northeast Louisiana. In Alaska, we pounded Alabama-Birmingham (92-64) and UMass (82-69) to earn a championship game berth against fourth-ranked North Carolina, which had Vince Carter and Antawn Jamison.

We led most of the way against the Tar Heels, but then in the final two minutes, the officials called an illegal screen against Cardinal and then an unbelievable intentional foul on Eldridge. North Carolina prevailed, 73-69. Those two calls just sunk our ship, which was frustrating. It seemed like North Carolina just had this hold over us. But even in defeat, I could see that this team was developing and really starting to come together.

We went from Alaska to the Great Eight in Chicago, where No. 7 ranked Kentucky beat us 89-75. From there, we went to Louisville and defeated them, which gave me my 372nd win at Purdue. That broke Purdue's school record for victories, set by legendary coach Ward "Piggy" Lambert, who was John Wooden's college coach at Purdue.

We continued to play well, beating No. 10 Xavier by a bucket and then Providence. We were 11-2 as we prepared for our December 30 Big Ten opener against Michigan State in Mackey Arena. That became one of the most frustrating late Decembers I've ever had. The Purdue football team was in San Antonio for the Alamo Bowl against Oklahoma State. We moved our starting time to early evening so that everyone could watch our basketball game and then go home and watch the football bowl game. Problem was, Tom Izzo forget to tell everyone that he had the makings of a potential National Championship team. Michigan State beat us 74-57. They really kicked our fannies that night. Morris Peterson had a great game. Our football team won the bowl game that night, but we did not hold up our end of the bargain.

Still, we bounced right back, beating Minnesota in Minneapolis to start a four-game winning streak. We won 11 of our next 12, with our only loss coming at Indiana (94-88).

We lost at Iowa and Penn State, came home and beat Minnesota, and then went to Michigan State for the regular-season finale. Michigan State had gone from unranked in our first meeting to ranked 10th by this meeting. Michigan State was going to win at least a share of the league championship, and they had a title banner rolled up at the top of the Breslin Center. We ended up beating them 99-96 in overtime. That probably was Brad Miller's best game ever. He had 30 points and double-figure rebounds in the win.

This became a special March for us because we were participating in the first Big Ten Conference tournament, which was staged in Chicago's United Center. Until that first conference tournament, I had been against a postseason conference tourney. But once we played in one, I changed my mind. I thought competing in a conference tournament helped us be battle-tested for the NCAA tournament. We were ranked ninth in the final poll and opened the league tournament with a victory against Indiana and then another against No. 17 Illinois, which put us in the title game against No. 18 Michigan and Robert "Tractor" Traylor. Michigan beat us 76-67, but it was learned several years later that many of those Michigan players should have been ineligible because of recruiting violations. That bothered me, because we should have won the title in the first Big Ten tournament.

The irony of the NCAA tournament that year is that we returned to Chicago and played first- and second-round games in the United Center, where we had played three times the previous week. We defeated Delaware (95-56) and Detroit (80-65) to advance to the Sweet Sixteen for the first time since 1994, when Glenn Robinson was in his final collegiate season. We were matched against No. 10 Stanford in St. Louis, and they ended our season with a 67-59 victory. Mark Madsen had a great game for Stanford, and we finished the year 28-8.

Stanford ended up going to the Final Four. They had more depth than we did, and they were a bigger team than we were. Madsen just beat the hell out of Brad Miller that night. Brad had cuts over his eye and a bloody nose. It was unbelievable that the referees were not calling fouls, but coach Mike Montgomery had said during the week leading into that game that Stanford would have to match the physical play of a Big Ten team—and they certainly did.

That loss marked the end of the careers of Brad and Chad, who really were good players for us for four years. They were kids who kind of flew under the recruiting radar. Those who compile recruiting services did not have Brad or Chad rated very high on the lists, which helped us land them. Brad may have been the best passer we ever had. When Brad was a freshman in high school, he was a point guard. But as he aged, he just grew and grew and grew, causing him to change into a center. He could shoot free throws and had an excellent touch around the basket. And he possessed a good knowledge of how to play the game.

Brad's only problem was that he hung around with a questionable group of guys from his hometown of Kendallville, Indiana. That may have kept him from being an All-American. I think he could have been a truly great college player if had he worked a little harder during the offseasons. Brad also is one of those kids who didn't like to eat breakfast, which I always told him is the day's most important meal. And it seemed like Brad always was almost academically ineligible before the start of each semester. But to his credit, he always made the cut. His mother and grandmother would be so angry

**Chad Austin provided our 1998 team with a third talented scorer. During that season—his senior year—he nailed 67 three-pointers and averaged 17 points a game for the second consecutive year.** *Purdue Sports Information*

with him, and then he would clamp down and make it. During his freshman year, they blamed me when he was almost ruled ineligible. They told me that I wasn't looking after Brad. I said, "Whoa, whoa, whoa!" Finally, they figured out that it was Brad's fault and not our fault.

Conversely, we never had to worry about Chad's grades. He was one of those players who always took care of business. We lost his older brother Woody to grades for one semester, but that was never an issue with Chad. Chad is one of the best three-point shooters to ever play at Purdue, and that was because he grew up with a basketball in his hands in Richmond, Indiana. Chad was always around the Purdue campus growing up, watching his brother Woody play. He's a true basketball junkie, and he benefited from learning under a very good high school coach in George Griffith. I don't know how else to explain Chad's success other than to say that he was a dedicated basketball player. Rick Majerus is one of the college coaches who just loved Chad after coaching him on that USA team that went to Australia in 1997.

With Brad and Chad and Brian Cardinal, that 1998 team was one of our best. But as good as that 1997-98 team was, it could have been even better had shooting guard Jaraan Cornell, who was a sophomore, not suffered a very bad high-ankle sprain in a February victory against Indiana in Mackey Arena. Indiana's Michael Lewis accidentally stepped on Jaraan's foot, and Jaraan really rolled his ankle. He was never the same that season. If he could have avoided that fluke injury, that team could have been something. He gave us an edge with his outside shooting, with Chad Austin on one wing and Jaraan on the other.

That bunch scored at least 100 points five times during the regular season, and often scored in the 90s, too. On February 7, 1998, we beat Ohio State 107-75 in Columbus in what was the best game that I coached at Purdue, especially considering that it was on the road. It was as if Brad, Chad, Brian, and Jaraan were playing a game on our home court. That also was the final time we played in old St. John Arena before the Buckeyes moved into Value City Arena. That night, I remember watching them play and thinking, "This is easy."

## CHAPTER THIRTEEN

# Transitioning into a New Century

The perception among fans and the national media heading into the 1998-99 season was that trouble lay ahead, even though we were ranked 16th heading into non-conference play. How would we replace Brad Miller and Chad Austin? Could Brian Cardinal, Jaraan Cornell, and Mike Robinson pick up additional scoring and rebounding slack? We entered the 1998-99 season with many questions to be answered and many expectations to be realized. In the end, that year was one of those seasons during which we made some noise in the NCAA tournament when no one really expected it.

The beginning of that season was extremely gratifying, because we were 12-1 and ranked eighth in the nation after defeating South Carolina 80-64 in December in the Jimmy V. Classic in New Jersey. Earlier we had qualified for the Preseason NIT Final Four in Madison Square Garden, where we lost in the semifinals to No. 10 North Carolina but then placed third by beating St. John's 70-69 on Cornell's last-second shot, which he banked in off the glass.

From there, we went to Providence and were beat 87-82 on a trip during which I was sicker than a dog. To make matters worse, referee Jim Burr gave me a technical foul in that game, but I deserved it. We also learned on that trip that Jamaal Davis, a 6-8 forward we had recruited out of Merrillville, Indiana, was academically ineligible for the second semester. No wonder I was sick.

After the Providence game, we began what would be a strange, up-and-down Big Ten Conference season. We won at Penn State (70-67) to open the season, but then lost at No. 24 Wisconsin. We also lost at Northwestern, but won on the road at Indiana and Illinois, which are extremely difficult places to play. Overall, our conference play was disappointing, as we finished 7-9 in the Big Ten. In the Big Ten tournament, we lost our opening-round game to Michigan (79-73) in overtime, which was a loss that got our attention as we prepared for the NCAA tournament. Our team re-focused after that game. The Big Ten tournament can work in two ways. If you lose and you are not supposed to get beat, it motivates you. It also can help a team get on a roll and bolster its confidence if it wins a lot in Big Ten tournament play.

We were placed in the East Regional's first- and second-round site at Boston. The trip to Boston was a highlight, in part because Bob Ryan, the terrific columnist for the *Boston Globe*, wrote a very complimentary column about me. I about fainted after I read it. We went out the next night and defeated an excellent Texas team 58-54 on a last-second shot by Cameron Stephens, a talented forward who experienced some academic problems and left us for UNC-Charlotte. The victory against Texas was impressive, because they had an excellent big man in Chris Mihm.

In the next round, we beat No. 2 seed and 10th-ranked Miami, Florida, 73-63. Miami was an extremely talented team, but our guys played a great first half, from which Miami never recovered. Then we moved into the Sweet Sixteen at The Meadowlands in East Rutherford, New Jersey, where we were beaten by Temple. The Owls' zone defense, which hurt us in the 1991 NCAA tournament, got us again in 1999. They beat us 77-55, which was embarassing. We finished the year 21-13.

The odd thing about a season such as 1998-99—a year loaded with pleasing victories—is that I went to the postseason banquet and ended up apologizing to fans. People do get spoiled. It was at that time that I began to feel that people were starting to lose interest in us if we did not come up with something great. In the 1980s and throughout part of the 1990s, we would win a big game on the road, and when we returned to campus, there would be lots of people to greet us. Those fans understood how huge it was to win on the road. But then in 1996 and again in 1997, for example, Chad Austin hit a last-second shot to beat Indiana in Bloomington, and when we arrived home, nobody showed up to meet us. By comparison, when Steve Scheffler and that group won at Indiana in 1990, there were several thousand fans outside Mackey Arena when we returned to campus.

In 1999, I could see the handwriting on the wall, and that probably was the time that I should have left Purdue. Had

I been smart, I would have. But again, I knew with Cardinal, Cornell, Robinson, and the rest of that group, we could have a good team in 1999-2000. There continued, however, to be lots of distractions. Mike Robinson always had something cooking. He didn't bother me, but I think he was bothering other guys more than we thought. Mike loves to talk, and I think that sometimes it just distracted his teammates. But to his credit, Mike had an excellent senior season for us.

The 1999-2000 squad finished the season 24-10 and ranked 23rd in the country, right where it began the year ranked. We kicked off the non-conference schedule at the Maui Invitational, where we beat Chaminade 96-78 and then played a wonderful game to beat sixth-ranked Florida 79-68. Fourth-ranked North Carolina defeated us 90-75 in the championship game, but the kids proved something to themselves in Hawaii.

As well as we played in Hawaii, we played every bit as poorly when we came home and lost to North Carolina State (61-59) in the ACC/Big Ten Challenge in Mackey Arena. Later in December, we had a two-game road swing through California, where we defeated Santa Clara (70-55) and then lost at No. 24 UCLA (55-53) when we allowed Jason Kapono to drive the length of the floor for a game-winning layup.

What a lot of people don't know about that trip is that after we defeated Santa Clara, Olympic soccer star Brandi Chastain came back to our locker room area and asked to meet me. Talk about a shock! I didn't know she even knew who I was. I had watched her team win the gold medal, which was great. I enjoyed her ability and spirit, and when she sought me out to tell me how much she enjoyed watching me coach and how much she enjoyed watching our teams play, I was extremely flattered. Her husband was a member of the coaching staff at Santa Clara, so I thought that whole scenario was kind of neat. That was a memorable trip overall, because Dick Davie, who was Santa Clara's coach, has been a good friend for many years.

During the 2000 Big Ten season, we stubbed our toes at Wisconsin and Ohio State, but won key games at Illinois and at home against No. 6 Michigan State. Beginning with a victory on February 2 at Northwestern, we won eight in a row and were ranked 20th when we went to Indiana for the final Big Ten regular-season game. Had we won the Indiana game, we would have earned a share of the Big Ten championship, but the Hoosiers, who were ranked 14th at the time, beat us 79-65.

I jumped on our colorful point guard, Carson Cunningham, pretty good in the locker room after the game. He just played out of control—wilder than a March hare. Carson is an intelligent young man and wanted to talk back to me. I had to leave the dressing room, because I was about to really get after him. Our athletic director, Morgan Burke, was in the locker room at that time, and had I gotten out of control, I might have been another Steve Green, who was the Purdue baseball coach who was fired for an unpleasant altercation with one of his players. I just had to get out of that locker room, cool down, and then come back. So I did.

From there we went to the Big Ten tournament and promptly lost to Wisconsin, 78-66. We had a 10-day layoff before that game against Wisconsin in the tournament, which hurt us. But again, a loss in the Big Ten tournament energized us for the NCAA tournament. We were assigned to the West Regional in Tucson, Arizona, where we won two very good games. We defeated Dayton 62-61, and then eliminated 12th-ranked Oklahoma 66-62 in the second round. In the Sweet Sixteen in Albuquerque, we beat Gonzaga 75-66. It was a key victory for us, as we played up to expectations.

After beating Gonzaga, we were within a game of a trip to Indianapolis and the Final Four. But we had to play Wisconsin for a fourth time that season, and they got us again, 64-60. It was our third loss in a row to the Badgers. I was happy for Wisconsin coach Dick Bennett, but I was so sad for our kids. Those players were characters, but the pieces of that puzzle fit together well. Cardinal. Cunningham. Mike Robinson. All of them were characters. Greg McQuay, our center, was kind of a hidden character. He is a fine artist and more of a character than many people thought.

Throughout my career at Purdue, I always told my friends that we would go to the Final Four during a season we did not expect it to happen. That 1999-2000 group could have been that team. It came very close to beating Wisconsin and earning a Final Four trip. Had we played anybody with the exception of Wisconsin in the West Regional final, we probably would have advanced. But Wisconsin just knew us so well. Mike Kelly, their great defensive guard, had Jaraan Cornell's number and shut him down. I've always said that matchups are the key to getting through the NCAA tournament.

I really wanted to take that team to the Final Four, in part because Brian Cardinal wanted to go to the Final Four in the worst way. It almost worked because Mike Robinson finally harnessed his talent and bought into what we were doing. Cardinal and McQuay weren't big, but they were battlers. Jaraan could shoot it, and Carson played very well in those NCAA tournament games. He handled the ball and took care of business.

While they were a collection of characters, that 1999-2000 team was not difficult to coach, because I got along with all of them very well. Mike Robinson may have been the most challenging, because he was always coming up with something. One time, we came into the dorm for a pregame meeting right before we were going to send the kids to bed, and Mike said, "I've got some bad news for you, Coach." I said, "What are you talking about?" Mike said, "Well, Rodney Smith has a girl in his room." I said, "You are telling me this? What the hell, are you a squealer?"

They were kind of competing for the small forward spot, and Mike must have figured that if I suspended Rodney, he wouldn't have any competition. I don't know why Mike would otherwise do that. What Mike should have done was pull Rodney aside and tell him not to do that any more so the coaches wouldn't find out about it. Instead, Mike came straight to me and told me. Right then, I think the Lord said, "This is the last time you are winning, Keady."

After the millennium, it was like our program was bitten by a snake. But the truth is, my last five teams were not good enough to win consistently. The 2000 NCAA West Regional championship game was the final time we really had an opportunity to do something special. I regret that, but it is the truth.

✦ ✦ ✦ ✦

David Letterman, who, by the way, is an Indianapolis native and a Ball State University graduate, asked me to be on his show in 2000. The story begins when we were playing in the first and second rounds of the 2000 NCAA tournament in

Tucson, Arizona. The television people there were making fun of my hair, and Letterman picked up on it. Soon after the season ended, someone from his show called our office and asked if I would be interested in going on David's show for a rebuttal of sorts by reading his famous Top 10 list.

At first I said no. We were on the road recruiting by that time, and I was feeling bad that we were defeated by Wisconsin in the NCAA tournament. I did not want to go on national television. I do enjoy television work, but appearing on the David Letterman Show is a much different experience than being in studio at CBS or ESPN to provide color commentary. I've had the opportunity to appear on ESPN with my former assistant Steve Lavin, and that was lots of fun. It's something that I would be interested in doing now that I have retired from Purdue.

Jim Vruggink, our sports information director at that time, was the one who wanted me to go on Dave's show. And my wife, Pat, talked me into it. So we got it set up so that I could make the trip to New York to appear on the David Letterman Show. Reading his Top 10 list wasn't as easy as you may think. The Top 10 is written on large cards, and I had to go into the studio and rehearse it. Plus, part of the list was an attempt to poke fun at my own hair, which seems to be a popular thing to do. But I pulled the reading off, and the experience was a lot of fun. Dave's band leader, Paul Shaffer, is a funny guy—as is Dave. He came over to me during commercials, shook my hand, and thanked me for taking his good-natured jabs at my hair in stride.

✦  ✦  ✦  ✦

In the summer of 2000, the NCAA concluded an investigation into our program that centered on the 1995-96 season, when we had forward Luther Clay as a member of our team. The NCAA handed down penalties, including the loss of a scholarship for two years and probation, because it said that we had arranged for illegal benefits for Luther, who came to us from Maine Central Institute Prep School and eventually left the program and transferred to Rhode Island. The thing that was so hard for me about the NCAA's findings is that it was not fair. It was not fair to our players. The NCAA never proved that we ever did anything wrong.

It seemed that the NCAA wanted to get something on our assistant coach, Frank Kendrick. Frank might have been guilty, but the NCAA never proved it. The only thing the NCAA proved was that while we were recruiting Jamaal Davis, Frank gave him a ride from Mackey Arena to the University Inn Hotel, which is only a mile along Northwestern Avenue from Mackey. Frank gave Jamaal a ride because Jamaal's mother was late picking him up. Frank was just trying to help the kid. If he had just told athletic director Morgan Burke that he had provided the ride, we might have gotten off the hook.

The whole thing hurt me very deeply, because Lin Dunn, our former women's basketball coach at Purdue, is the individual who turned in the allegations to the NCAA. She is the person who got the whole thing started. I would have preferred that Lin bring it to me so that I could have self-reported it. But she went behind my back because she was trying to get to Morgan. He had not renewed Lin's contract, and she was bitter.

People ask, "Should you have recruited Luther Clay and Jamaal Davis?" Well, Luther was a great talent, but he hurt his knee in the Five-Star Camp before his senior year, and that jolted him. I don't know what happened then, but he had a lot of stuff going on in his personal life that he could not handle. He did not have much help in terms of a family. Luther expected favors. Then we had the investigation, and we wanted to clear our names. We wanted to make sure that people knew that we didn't cheat at Purdue. But from the get-go, the NCAA told me that I was not involved in any of it. So I said, "Then why are we doing this?"

Morgan Burke, Purdue University President Steven Beering, Frank Kendrick, and I were called to Virginia to testify before an NCAA committee. It was agonizing to have to go through all the questioning and listen to people speak. The other thing that really upset me was that the NCAA's investigative team was headed up by an Indiana University graduate. Then, one of the Fort Wayne newspapers published an article about all the phone numbers that were dialed from the men's basketball office. All they ever proved was that I made a call to Jamaal Davis's mother's candy distribution center to purchase one box of peanut clusters. His mother sold candy for a living. But that was not going to influence Jamaal to come to Purdue. It was a $10 candy sale.

When we were sanctioned, it hurt me, but I think it really hurt the whole program. It set us back. I think the sanctions—along with my age—severely hurt our recruiting. The other thing they began to use against me in recruiting is that players were told, "Keady has been close to getting to the Final Four, but he never has gotten there." People were not satisfied that we graduate our players, win 20 games almost every year, and had won six Big Ten Conference championships. Fans wanted us to go to the Final Four. Once the NCAA sanctions came down, fans became disenchanted with our program. On top of that, we played poorly after the 2000 season. We were not a lot of fun to watch.

## CHAPTER FOURTEEN

# Striking Gold

From the time I was a kid, I've enjoyed Olympic competition. Basketball, track and field, boxing—you name it, and I've watched it. Never did I think I would have the opportunity to be involved in the Olympics. However, my dream became reality during the 2000 Summer Olympic Games when I served as an assistant coach for the gold-medal-winning men's basketball team in Sydney, Australia.

My journey was a long yet very rewarding one, certainly something I never will forget. In fact, I think about it probably once a day. My journey to the Olympics had humble beginnings. In 1979, I had the opportunity to coach the South team to a gold medal in the National Sports Festival in Colorado, which is where former Purdue coach Fred Schaus saw me and liked the way I coached. That was my first USA Basketball experience, and it was the beginning of several wonderful international experiences for me.

In 1984, Bob Knight asked me to assist in the selection of the United States Olympic team, which captured the gold medal. Former Michigan and Iowa State coach Johnny Orr and I were roommates in Bloomington, Indiana, as we helped Bob put together our Olympic squad. That was an enjoyable experience, although when I tell people we cut former NBA standouts Terry Porter, John Stockton, and Charles Barkley, they look at me with great surprise.

In 1985, USA Basketball asked me to take a United States Olympic Developmental team to Taiwan. My Purdue players Troy Lewis and Todd Mitchell were members of that team. Current Michigan coach Tommy Amaker, who was a standout at Duke, also was on that team. I thoroughly enjoyed coaching Tommy. He is really one of those good guys. We were there for 16 days for the R. Williams Jones Cup Tournament, in which we claimed the silver medal with a 6-1 record.

Again in 1988, I was asked to help with Olympic team selections. Former St. John's coach Lou Carnesecca and I were roommates and helped John Thompson pick the team. I was at it again in 1989, taking our World University Games team to Germany, where we did win the gold, finishing 6-0. Purdue players Steve Scheffler and Tony Jones were members of that team.

Next I was picked to coach our Pan American Games team in Cuba in 1991. That team also would have won the gold, but former Ohio State standout Jimmy Jackson broke a foot in our fourth game, and Puerto Rico defeated us in the semifinals when Jimmy could not play. Christian Laettner, Grant Hill, and Tommy Hill from Duke were members of that team. We had a really good team, winning the bronze medal with a 6-1 mark.

From there, I was placed on a committee whose task it is to select USA Basketball players. A thrilling day in my life took place in February, 1999, when I was in Albuquerque, New Mexico, giving a motivational speech. That night, I received a call from USA Basketball asking if I would consider being an assistant coach for the 2000 Olympic Games with Rudy Tomjanovich, Larry Brown, and Tubby Smith.

Our Olympic team played in the qualifying tournament in Puerto Rico. Rudy was ill and did not coach, so Larry was our head coach, and Tubby Smith and I were the assistants. The team went 10-0 to qualify for the Olympic Games in Sydney, Australia. This was a great team that included Tim Duncan, Kevin Garnett, Gary Payton, and Jason Kidd. Talk about talent. Man, that was fun. Our entire experience in Puerto Rico was enjoyable.

Then in 2000, we traveled to the Olympics. The experience was enhanced because my wife, Pat, got to travel with us. She always has been a warrior in terms of traveling with me. She made the trip to Puerto Rico for the Olympic qualifier the year before during a time when she was sick. In 2000, she felt much better.

We began our Olympic quest in Maui, where we took the team to practice for a week. The weather was great, and obviously, it is just so beautiful there. We took a short flight to Honolulu and played an exhibition game before departing for Japan, where we played exhibition games against Spain and Japan. From there, it was on to Melbourne, Australia, where we played the Australian team. Finally, it was on to Sydney. Our team went 8-0 in winning the gold medal. Croatia gave us a hell of a game, and we almost got beat. Then, we defeated France in the gold-medal game. Garnett, Payton, and Kidd played well, as did Ray Allen and Vince Carter.

This truly was a great experience. The travel was fun, especially considering the company we were keeping. The players were easy to coach. We never had a single problem. One of the special moments in my life occurred as I walked into the Olympic Stadium as a part of the opening ceremonies. You cannot imagine how magnificent it is when you walk in waving your country's flag. That opening ceremony in Sydney was unbelievable.

One of the fascinating aspects about being a member of the United States men's basketball Olympic team is the security that surrounds the team. Once we arrived in Sydney, our team stayed in a hotel. We were not housed in the Olympic Village. Five hours before the beginning of the Opening Ceremonies, our group walked to one of the arenas, where we visited in one of the lounge areas. We were asked to do that for security purposes. Tennis superstars Venus and Serena Williams were with us, as was then-first daughter Chelsea Clinton and Microsoft giant Bill Gates. We had our picture taken with Ms. Clinton and had an enjoyable time visiting with her. She is a very nice person and was familiar with our team. She either was very well informed about our team, or she really is a sports fan.

The Olympic experience was loaded with interesting stories. While we were staying in Melbourne, a large group of 5,000 or more protesters gathered outside the hotel where our basketball traveling party was staying. They were protesting

**Being on the sidelines during the 2000 Olympics with Larry Brown (left), Tubby Smith (right), and Rudy Tomjanovich (standing) was both a thrill and an honor.**
*Mike Hewitt/Getty Images*

against Nike's labor policies and the state of the world economy. We were told that some of them were paid protesters who had come from all over the world. In order to avoid any possible confrontation as we departed for Sydney, we had to leave at 5 a.m. Security was so tight that guards actually boarded our bus to make sure that we really were the Olympic team.

Before that, Larry Brown, Tubby Smith, and I had to leave the hotel for the purpose of staging a basketball clinic for a group of high school and club team coaches. The three of us actually had to sneak away from the hotel on a boat through a channel. The protesters observed us as we passed under a bridge. They were yelling and waving their flags at us, but fortunately, no one threw objects at us. When we came back in, there was no incident.

During competition, it was fun to be around the coaches from the other teams. I knew most of them from competition in other international events. The Chinese were impressive with four seven-footers. However, they have yet to refine their game. France had gotten a lot better, and Croatia was really good. With Olympic competition in this era, the main thing I've noticed is that fundamentals among U.S. opponents have improved dramatically. Sometimes, our players have a tendency to underestimate teams from other countries. But because Larry Brown, Tubby Smith, and I have had extensive foreign coaching experience, we told our players, "Hey, these guys are good. They can beat us if we are not ready to play." I think that helped our team focus. Even though our team members are NBA stars, we practiced a lot. In fact, we had to drive approximately 30 miles to reach our practice gymnasium. It was, however, all worth it when we won the gold medal.

We were proud to have won a gold for America. However, we did feel the pressure. Rudy said he would never do it again because it involved too much pressure, especially considering the coaches are not paid, other than our expenses. But an experience such as this one was priceless. And don't get me wrong. We had a great time. It was fun to discover that Jason Kidd and Ray Allen are avid golfers just like I am. Rudy,

Larry, Tubby, Quinn Buckner, and I played golf almost every day if there was a course nearby.

For me, it was a wonderful climax to more than 20 years of USA Basketball involvement, dating back to the National Sports Festival in 1979 when I was the head coach at Western Kentucky. Had I not coached that team, former Purdue coach Fred Schaus may not have observed me, and I might not have gotten the opportunity to be at Purdue for 25 seasons. It's amazing sometimes how life's twists and turns pan out. I guess I was in the right place at the right time in 1979.

✦ ✦ ✦ ✦

Another Olympic-related relationship I have nurtured is a great friendship with 1984 Olympic gold medalist Michael Jordan. I met Michael in 1984, when he was voted college basketball's Player of the Year, and I was voted Coach of the Year. That summer, Michael helped our Olympic team—coached by Bob Knight—win the gold.

I now have the opportunity to spend part of each August with Michael in Las Vegas, where I am one of the coaches for the Michael Jordan Basketball Fantasy Camp, which is staged at The Mirage right on the Vegas Strip. It's amazing to be surrounded by legendary coaches. Dean Smith. John Thompson. Tubby Smith. Eddie Sutton. Roy Williams. All of those guys are there to coach, and naturally, I've gotten closer to them because we are around each other every day.

But another reason I enjoy the camp so much is because I like spending time with the campers, who pay $15,000 each to participate. They are great guys. It's interesting, because it is just like coaching your own players at Purdue. The exception is, most of these participants are in their 40s and 50s and are

**Michael Jordan and I have been friends since 1984, when I was named Coach of the Year and he was named Player of the Year. Today, I help out at the Michael Jordan Basketball Fantasy Camp, which is a fun experience for both the campers and the celebrity coaches.** *Purdue Sports Information*

millionaires. I will yell at them often, but they love it, because many of them have never been talked to that harshly. Most of them are CEOs of their respective companies. The campers and the coaches eat together at breakfast and again at lunch. Then, we play games, so I am coaching 10 of them all the time. I've gotten to know many of them, because a lot of them come back again and again.

Most of the participants I coach in Michael's camp still play in organized leagues or at the YMCA in their hometowns. All of them are in good shape for their age. Several of them are in their 60s and have attended for nine years, which is how long I've been involved through Michael's request.

Michael is always around. He comes and lectures every day, then has fun with the guys by letting them go one-on-one with him. He may lecture on free-throw shooting one day, three-point shooting the next, and then the art of developing a jump shot. In 2004, he had Jerry West, John Wooden, and John Thompson as guest speakers.

My favorite Michael Jordan Fantasy Camp story centers on one of my former Purdue players—guard Curt Clawson, who attended for the first time in 2003. Curt is now an executive for a large company in Michigan. I wanted Curt on my team, but because we draw for our draft choices it wasn't up to me. Since Curt was a former Big Ten player, he was already gone by the time I picked at No. 8. That year, Michael staged an around-the-world shooting contest and made eight or nine out of 10. Then Michael said, "If anybody here makes every shot, he gets free tuition for 2004." Curt Clawson made all 10 shots. I think that speaks volumes of how good Curt Clawson still is more than 20 years after playing his final collegiate game, and it speaks volumes about what a good, fun-loving guy Michael Jordan is.

Michael Jordan is among the greatest guys I know. His biggest asset is his character. I knew that about him in 1984 when we went to CBS to tape the Player and Coach of the Year awards show. Michael really likes my wife, Pat. He said, "How in the heck did you get her, Keady?" Michael always has been great fun to be around because he is so genuine.

The Fantasy Camp begins with a golf outing at Shadow Creek. The next day, we watch the campers play on five courts at The Mirage in order to determine their talent. They go through a series of drills for an hour. Then at 6 p.m., we go into a room and stage our draft, which is a lot of fun. The next day, we start playing games, listen to Michael's first lecture, and put the campers through more stations in which we instruct. I may have passing one year. Another year, I taught the pick-and-roll. The games don't last very long, because we don't want to kill the campers.

Our referees come from the Atlantic Coast Conference, and the games usually are extremely competitive. We stage a pool-play format to determine where a team is placed in our tournament. To win the tournament, a team must win four games in one day, so players with endurance are a priority.

On the last night, we have a ceremony during which we present the awards. It's five days of togetherness with these guys, most of whom get to know the UNLV athletic trainer very well. That guy has seen it all, from guys breaking legs on the first day to knees going out. The training room is packed after the third day. But what a great time it is, thanks to Michael Jordan—a dear friend and great ambassador for basketball and for our nation.

## CHAPTER FIFTEEN

# Me and Bob Knight

The year 2000 was full of strange twists, including the firing of Bob Knight by then-Indiana University president Myles Brand. It took place in September, when I was at the Olympic Games, serving as an assistant coach. At the time of Bob's firing, I was upset about it, but I was more interested in trying to get our 2000-01 team going. But about a year later, I was really sad about losing Bob. It was a sad time for the great era of Indiana basketball, because Indiana kids grew up either disliking Knight or disliking me. The rivalry was not the same from 2000-01 through my last season in 2004-05. For years and years throughout the country, everybody said that Purdue-Indiana was the best college basketball rivalry. Now you don't hear anyone outside the state of Indiana talk about it. It is not even considered a good rivalry any more. But Matt Painter will get it back there.

For me, it was fun to try to beat the best. That is how I looked at it. Bob Knight is a great coach. Just like John Wooden's great UCLA teams, Bob Knight's Indiana and Texas Tech teams were and are very fundamentally sound. They take good shots. And in the early 1980s they played damn good defense. Then for a while Bob adopted more of an offensive scheme. It's difficult to maintain hard-nosed defensive strategies as a coach, because it takes a lot out of you. To do it, the head coach must maintain his intensity, and his coaching staff also has to stay intense.

Our battles were great. I don't know that I would say that I loved coaching against him, but I certainly looked forward to it. When you beat a Bob Knight-coached team, you feel like you have achieved something special, and your alumni are happy, too. If we beat Indiana, it always helped our standing with the NCAA tournament selection committee.

But late in Bob's tenure at Indiana, he didn't have a lot of great players. Now that he is at Texas Tech, his athletes are a lot better than the ones he had during his final years at Indiana. That's why Texas Tech is winning.

I think something else that needs to be noted here is that it always will be difficult for the head basketball coach at Purdue and the head basketball coach at Indiana to be good friends. In fact, I don't think you can be. There are just certain things you cannot say to each other. The Purdue coach cannot compliment the IU coach. The Purdue coach certainly can respect Indiana's coach, which I did. He can say that Indiana's coach outcoached him in a particular game, which I did. But he can't do that for very long, since it's such a big rivalry.

For a while, Bob and I were about as close as you can be, especially when you take into consideration his temperament, my temperament, and the rivalry. He asked me to help him with the 1984 U.S. Olympic team, and I got pretty close to Bob's sons, Tim and Patrick, when they were little boys. In fact, Tim tried to get me to wear a red shirt when we played an All-Star team in Indianapolis. There wasn't any way I was going to wear a U.S. Olympic shirt that was red. Tim laughed and said, "I almost got you, didn't I, Coach?"

I guess I can't write about our relationship and my rivalry with Coach Knight without discussing our game on February 23, 1985, in Bloomington's Assembly Hall. In our 72-63 victory, in what has become a famous scene, Bob tossed a chair across the court as our guard Steve Reid stepped to the line to shoot technical foul free throws. We had an 11-point lead at the time Bob picked up the chair. It didn't surprise me when he threw it, because I knew he was angry. Had it been any other coach, it would have surprised me. But with Bob, it did not surprise me. I still think it was premeditated. I think he wanted to take the attention away from us.

He is notorious for doing anything he can to take attention away from Purdue. One time, he brought a donkey onto the set of his television show and said the donkey was a typical Purdue representative. Another time, he said our cheerleaders displayed unsportsmanlike conduct. It was always something with him, which tickled me, because he always was trying to center attention on Indiana instead of centering that attention on a Purdue victory. We won about half the games we played against his Indiana teams.

In the "chair toss" game, we were playing pretty well, and for once in Bloomington, the referees were calling the game fairly, as I saw it. We were getting a little bit of a lead. We had a good team that year. Steve went to the free throw line, and the next thing I knew, the chair went flying across the floor. Bob was ejected, and Steve missed three of the six technical foul free throws. I really chewed Steve's butt for missing those free throws. I told him, "If we lose this game, it is going to be your fault." I probably also told him that if we lost, he would be walking home to West Lafayette, which is 112 miles from Bloomington. I was always saying stuff like that. But even after the chair was tossed, our kids continued to play well, and we won. Honestly, the incident did not seem to distract our guys. We maintained focus, which is a credit to a pretty disciplined basketball team.

People often ask if that's the craziest thing that I've seen in coaching, and the answer has to be yes. In the aftermath of that victory, another crazy thing happened. Our next game was at Illinois, and they beat us 86-43. It is a Purdue tradition that on the bus trip back from Champaign to West Lafayette, we stop at the Beef House Restaurant near Covington, Indiana, and pick up these wonderful pork tenderloin sandwiches for our players. I was so angry after that loss that I, too, threw something. I picked up that box of tenderloins and threw them all in the ditch.

I got back on the bus and told our players, "We are not eating. We are going home and practicing." We got to Mackey Arena and practiced until 3 a.m.

# CHAPTER SIXTEEN

# Bruised and Battered

As the century turned, it seemed as if there was a turn-of-the century attitude change in players and their parents. Of course, it's easy now to look back on that and make those kinds of observations, but at that time—the start of the 2000-01 season—we thought the gun was loaded, so let's get ready to fire away. But that was not the case. The members of that team did not want to put the time, effort, or attitude into doing what the previous 20 teams had done. I don't think they took pride in the tradition the players before them had established. I don't know what caused that change, because we certainly were not doing anything different in our teaching.

I thought Rodney Smith, John Allison, and Maynard Lewis really were going to be a nice nucleus for our 2000-01 team. We had Carson Cunningham coming back as a starter from our NCAA tournament Elite Eight team, and he really had played well in games against Dayton and Oklahoma in the NCAA tournament. We also added Joe Marshall, a transfer from Mississippi State. I thought we were going to have pretty good depth. But injuries riddled us that season.

Within one week during the Big Ten season, Rodney Smith, our starting forward, and John Allison, our starting center, each suffered a stress fracture of the foot. That set us back, because those young men really needed to play, and they really needed to be hungry. I'm convinced those injuries set Rodney and John back for the 2001-02 season, too. It seemed to me as if their injuries became the footnote for our final five seasons at Purdue. Later, Kenneth Lowe got hurt and Andrew Ford sustained a shoulder injury. Just when it appeared we might get going, someone would suffer an injury.

My final Purdue team, which finished 7-21, had all kinds of injuries, too. David Teague broke a hand, Bryant Dillon sustained a serious knee injury, and Carl Landry, our leading scorer, also suffered a season-ending knee injury in late February. Those things happen, but Purdue had always been a program that had overcome obstacles and overachieved. I really thought we had good players in 2000-01, but as I look back on it, I realize that they were good players, but they also played above their ability. Beginning with that season, we ceased to play above our ability—and that hurt us.

We were good enough to win, but when a team does not win, I always blame myself. I ask myself, "Why wasn't I more motivated?" Or, "Why wasn't I teaching better?" Or, "Why wasn't I recruiting better?" My competitive spirit always took over, and I would say, "We can fix this!" Well, we were not going to fix it. The players had to realize that it was broken and then want to fix it.

My philosophy on coaching has also changed. I have thought long and hard to come to the conclusion that coaching can only take a program so far. To achieve success, everyone else has to want it more than I want it. I asked myself, "What has the administration done to help me win?" I'm not sure they were doing much during my final five years at Purdue. I think the administration had other goals in mind, such as getting Joe Tiller's football program really going, along with some other sports.

It really bothered me that we did poorly the last five years, winning 73 games and losing 79, making only one NCAA tournament appearance (in 2003) and experiencing two sub-.500 seasons. I do not believe that there was that same commitment to get us to that next level. I think a basketball practice facility should have been built. We need a players' lounge at Purdue. And I don't think that it's just us. I think other sports need it, too. I think that these things will come in time.

But what I really believe above all else is that Purdue needed a new men's basketball coach. I had run my quarter-mile, and I had nothing left. That's the best test of how much intestinal fortitude someone has—running 400 meters. To translate that into coaching terms, in 2000-01, we did not do a good job setting a foundation for the next three or four years. I kept thinking, "We are going to get this fixed." But it wasn't going to be fixed. What happened during my last five years at Purdue bothers me a lot. I know that some people think I was never able to recruit well, but they are full of you know what. We had 16 All-Big Ten players here. So don't tell me that I can't recruit.

Even as we struggled to a 17-15 record in 2000-01, we showed signs of life. We beat No. 1-ranked Arizona 72-69 in the John Wooden Tradition in Indianapolis, and we played well in the NIT, beating Illinois State and Auburn before losing in double-overtime to Alabama. Had we beaten Alabama, we would have gone to the NIT's Final Four in New York. But we failed to finish the game against Alabama. That was part of the syndrome that plagued us near the end of my Purdue career. The plays we had made in previous years—plays that made us winners—were not being made. In my first five years at Purdue, we lost only 10 games decided by four points or less. In my final five years at Purdue, we lost 17 games decided by four points or less. Obviously, there is a mentality there that changed. I hope it wasn't mine.

As frustrating as the 2000-01 season was, the 2001-02 campaign was even more frustrating. A lot of negative stuff was going on with our seniors. Rodney Smith didn't want to play. Something happened to him that lessened his passion for basketball. Then John Allison's mother told everyone seated in the good seats we call "The Pit" that we were a poor coaching staff. It ended up being a bad mix of players after we thought it was going to be a great mix. When I recruited Rodney, John, and Maynard Lewis, I thought they were going to be a productive nucleus with good attitudes. They weren't bad kids, but they were not fighters or competitors. They really didn't want to win as badly as someone like Brian Cardinal wanted to win. We always made certain that we had great families backing our players. Mothers and fathers were always special to us. But that

Our 72-69 victory over No. 1-ranked Arizona in the John Wooden Tradition in 2000 was a reason to celebrate in a year full of ups and downs. *AP/WWP*

changed during my last five years. I began to need to schedule parent meetings.

I'm not trying to place the focus for our problems on them, but our program had fallen into that type of mix with all of our players. It all crashed down upon us in 2001-02, when we were 13-18, capped by a season-ending 87-72 loss to Iowa in the Big Ten tournament in Indianapolis.

When that season ended, I felt like I had failed everyone. I had failed the players, because I didn't teach them correctly. I had failed the fans, who were disgruntled when we don't win. I also think the fans had left us when we didn't go to the Final Four in 2000. It was as if they said, "Well, Keady has had his chance, and he didn't get there. So, we will go support someone else."

I don't think the fans had let us down, though; I think we let our fans down. Had we gone to the 2000 Final Four, maybe we could have done better these past few seasons. This kind of thing happens all over the country. People are not going to support teams that don't play themselves into championship situations. A lot of fans hung with us, but some did not.

You just cannot imagine how hard we worked at Purdue; when we failed, it was totally frustrating. When we had a losing record in 1989, I knew it was because we had a lot of poor attitudes on the team. The 2001-02 team was aware of our basketball family philosophy but didn't really care about it.

Before the 2002-03 season, we took the team on a European tour, and it set a solid tone for what would be a 19-11 record and our final trip to the NCAA tournament, where we defeated LSU in the first round before losing a tough game to No. 5 Texas. In Europe, we had an opportunity to be with that team and to do a lot of bonding. Willie Deane, a guard who had transferred to Purdue from Boston College, and I, got to talk a lot as we would walk from place to place. We talked about things like how to deal with referees and what to say and what not to say. Willie was a special talent, but for some reason I got the feeling that he thought we did not like him. I like all of my players, and I really liked Willie. We were just trying to help him become a better player.

We also added Chris Booker to that 2002-03 team, which helped us a lot. Chris was a 6-10 center who really could play. We had another big man, 6-11 Ivan Kartelo, who we could not take on our European tour because he was caught cheating on a first-semester final examination. I should have cut him right there. That would have set the tone for everybody else. But I always thought, "No, I'm going to help this kid."

We have rules, but we got to a point where our senior leadership was not demanding that we enforce the rules that were in place. All through the years, our seniors had demanded that.

Despite our problems, more injuries included in that mix, we fought through things and got into the NCAA tournament. Melvin Buckley, a kid we thought really would help us before he left to go to South Florida, had a great game against LSU, helping us to win our first NCAA tournament contest since 2000. In the next round, we competed against Texas, and that's all a coach can ask. Texas just beat us.

We thought that maybe we were back on track after that season, and we were until Chris Booker became academically ineligible after the first semester of the 2003-04 season. If a player of mine ever takes Portuguese again, I'm going to kill him. Chris took that foreign language class and failed the course. Seriously, he should have taken care of business.

In November 2003, before we lost Booker to grades, we experienced what probably was the highlight of my final two seasons at Purdue. We participated in the Great Alaska Shootout and won it, defeating a good Seton Hall team in the semifinals and then beating No. 2-ranked Duke 78-68 in the title game in Anchorage.

In the championship game, we took Duke by surprise. I think they were surprised by how well we guarded them. We did a pretty good job preparing for them as far as strategy was concerned. And we also caught a break in that we had a day off during the tournament and they did not. That helped us recuperate. The gentleman who was our team host in Alaska that year was very ill, and we kind of won the tournament for him. He passed away a few months later.

While there weren't a lot of highlights during our final five years at Purdue, it made me feel great after the Duke victory when my good friend Mike Krzyzewski said during his press conference that Purdue was fortunate to have me as its coach. Naturally, when a guy of Mike's caliber says something like that, it makes me feel as if I have accomplished something during my career in the coaching world. Really, that's what it is all about—earning your colleagues' respect. College basketball fans really don't know me, although after reading this book they'll have a better idea of who I am. If they judge me based only on my scowl, they have misjudged me. Coming from Mike, that was a great compliment.

As I recall our Great Alaska Shootout trips, we played in that event four times, and posted a 10-2 record, with both losses coming to North Carolina. We won the event in 1993 and again in 2003. Our teams always seemed to play well there. The tournament is played early in the season when everyone is fighting to earn a position, so maybe our players played harder as a result. I always enjoyed our Great Alaska Shootout experiences, and so did Pat. The last one certainly was a lot of fun.

At one point in my next-to-last season, we were 8-1 and ranked 17th in the polls. That's when we learned that Booker might be in academic hot water, and our team was not as focused as it should have been. We lost by a point to Southern Methodist in the championship game of our Boilermaker Invitational, and that was the beginning of our slide. Two games later, we lost at Colorado State in a game in which they made two three-pointers in the final seconds for a 71-69 victory. The last three-pointer clearly came after the clock hit 0.00, but because the game was not televised, the officiating crew could not review the play.

Booker did not make the trip to Colorado State and then onto Baylor, where we won. But I think his loss affected the entire team. We kept battling and won a few games early in the Big Ten season, but then we experienced more injuries. Distractions that year were like a chain reaction that would never end. Kenneth Lowe injured his elbow in a game at Indiana. Matt Kiefer injured his foot at Michigan State. And after we won a big game at Minnesota, we returned to campus, and Ivan Kartelo went out that night to a bar and was arrested after getting into an altercation.

Suddenly a team that was 14-4 after beating Michigan State on January 25 lost 10 of its final 13 games, including an NIT defeat at Notre Dame to finish 17-14. As it turned out, that loss at Notre Dame was almost my final game as Purdue's head coach.

## CHAPTER SEVENTEEN

# My Heart was Almost in San Francisco

At the end of the 2003-04 season—my 24th at Purdue—I was tempted to leave for a coaching opportunity at the University of San Francisco, the school where former Boston Celtic greats Bill Russell and K.C. Jones won a pair of NCAA tournament championships in the mid-1950s. It was the second time in less than 10 years that my name was linked to the USF job. In the late 1990s, I interviewed for the University of San Francisco job with athletic director Bill Hogan, with whom I developed a friendship when Bill was the athletic director at St. Joseph's College in Rensselaer, Indiana, about 45 minutes north of West Lafayette. They ended up hiring Phil Mathews in the late 90s, but that was a job that intrigued me.

Pat always wanted to live in the San Francisco Bay area, and Bill often reminded me how much he liked the way I handled listeners who called into my weekly radio show. He said that was one of his highlights when he thought of me, and I said, "But what about the way I coach?"

Pat and I went out there for my interview in the late '90s. I was spotted on the San Francisco campus, and my presence was leaked to a writer for one of the San Francisco newspapers. The man who spotted me was the former junior college coach of Dean Garrett, who was the center for Bob Knight's 1987 NCAA championship team at Indiana. Anyway, after the story broke that I was interviewing for the USF job, I was angry, and I said, "I'm not interviewing for the San Francisco job." Otherwise, I might have taken the job seven or eight years ago.

At that time, I felt like we needed to step up our facilities at Purdue if we were ever going to get anywhere. And after 16 or 17 years at Purdue, I was looking to go somewhere where the weather is a little bit nicer than it is in Indiana. I thought we had paid our dues at Purdue. But I loved it there as well, so ultimately we didn't want to leave.

When the USF job opened again in the spring of 2004, I thought about it. I really wasn't interested in a contract extension at Purdue. I wanted athletic director Morgan Burke to say that a contract extension was going to be given, but I wasn't going to take it. I had decided that I did not want to further damage our recruiting.

I like Bill Hogan, and I like the people at San Francisco. I thought that job was a great opportunity, but we could not work out a housing deal. I would have taken the San Francisco job if they could have gotten me a house, because homes are just so expensive out there. Pat wanted to go to San Francisco but only if we received the desired housing arrangement. Pat is not a fool. You don't leave one job, take another, and then lose money in the process. The San Francisco job was also appealing because my sister, Norma, lives in Sacramento, California. Our good friends, Tom and Marilyn Meadors, live just above Oakland, California in Brentwood. We would have had our closest friends and my sister right there with us. It was kind of an ideal situation. We would have stayed there and retired.

I liked the San Francisco players when I interviewed them while I was out there. Those guys, who would have played for me, did well in 2004-05, getting into the NIT. At the same time, I thought the players at Purdue needed a new voice. I was wearing thin on them. I don't think today's generation of player is motivated by enthusiasm or by a coach simply getting after them. Today's player wants to be pampered by his coach. I don't think today's player likes or appreciates the intensity that I bring to the environment.

As the San Francisco saga was playing out in the spring of 2004, I had a closed-door meeting with our Purdue team. There was so much speculation about what was going to be said in that meeting. TV crews from throughout Indiana, and sports writers from almost every daily paper in our state flocked to Mackey on that rainy Friday afternoon. The leak was that during that meeting, I would tell our players that I was leaving. I wanted to set that record straight. The meeting was only to inform our players that I had not taken the San Francisco job yet, but as soon as I knew, I would tell them. I told the players that one way or the other, there would be no beating around the bush in regard to this situation. I wanted to let our players know exactly where I stood.

Reports circulated that I was prepared to tell them that I was going to San Francisco, and a couple of them talked me out of it. That also is not true. No one said anything to me. I don't think players today really care who their coach is. Point guard Brandon McKnight wanted me to stay for his senior year, but Brandon did not voice his opinion in that meeting. After the fact—days later—a couple players told me that they were glad that I decided to stay for my 25th year, but it wasn't like it was a big emotional thing. No one shed any tears.

We walked out of that closed-door meeting, and I still did not know what I was going to do. Funny thing is, all the reporters thought my mind was made up as I left that day, and they were wrong. I sought the advice of my agent, Dennis Coleman, who is our attorney for the National Association of Basketball Coaches. When the San Francisco situation came down to the final few negotiating points, Dennis was the only person talking with USF. I was not talking with them. He came into my room and could see that I was wavering—that I was not convinced I wanted to leave Purdue. He told me, "Keady, your heart is not in San Francisco. Go back and finish it at Purdue next year and then retire."

San Francisco did officially offer me the job. In fact, I still carry a copy of the contract in my briefcase. The financial package USF was offering was not that great, but I was happy with it. But the housing issue would have made striking a deal impossible. Not just difficult, but impossible.

While I'm offering up details about the San Francisco situation, I might as well say that I was also offered the San Diego State job near the turn of the century when Rick Bay was the athletic director there. He ended up hiring former Michigan coach Steve Fisher. Bay also tried to hire me when he was athletic director at Ohio State during the late 1980s. I liked the San Diego State situation because I liked Rick Bay, who like me, is a New York Yankees fan. There also was talk linking me to UNLV several years ago, but I was never offered that job.

✦ ✦ ✦ ✦

One thing people have to understand is that because I started coaching Division I basketball so late in my overall coaching career, I did not have a lot of money saved like many of today's young coaches. It took me a while in my career to start making good money. We worked for peanuts for a lot of years. So one of the reasons that I worked these past few years is that I really needed the money. It wasn't like I could just retire from coaching when I wanted to. The other factor was that I didn't want to retire. I have been in good health, and I still enjoy coaching. Plus, I love Purdue.

When Morgan Burke saw that I was serious about possibly leaving Purdue, he decided to ask me, "Who would you hire here at Purdue as your successor? We could bring that coach in for one year to work as your assistant, and then he could take over." With the San Francisco rumors finally put to rest, Morgan and I began to focus on the transition that eventually would bring Matt Painter to Purdue as our next head coach. We discussed several prominent names as options. At that point, Bruce Weber was established at Illinois, and we knew that Bruce was not going to come back. That is what I wanted to have happen in 2003. I wanted to bring Bruce back from Southern Illinois. But because of my contract, Bruce would have had to be my assistant for two seasons. That wasn't an ideal situation for him.

**I got the guy I wanted when former Purdue player Matt Painter agreed to become my successor at Purdue.** *Purdue Sports Information*

Steve Lavin, my former graduate assistant in the late 1980s who went on to do a great job at UCLA before moving on to ESPN as its excellent college basketball analyst, was also discussed as a possible replacement. But Morgan wasn't that interested in Steve. Vanderbilt's Kevin Stallings was another, but I thought Kevin really was set at Vanderbilt. If he moved along, I thought he would try to get a better job, something like Ohio State, which is a bigger job than Vanderbilt. I did not want to mess that up for Kevin. We also talked about Creighton's Dana Altman.

We ended up bringing Matt Painter—who was coaching at Southern Illinois during the 2003-04 season—on board to be my successor at Purdue. The interview process with Matt Painter, Morgan Burke, and me went very smoothly. Then the Purdue president gave us his okay. During a four-hour window on a weekend in April, 2004, we got everything worked out. I would return for my 25th and final year at Purdue with Matt at my side to be the next head coach. In the end, I got the guy I wanted. I hope it works out well for Matt and for everyone at Purdue.

## CHAPTER EIGHTEEN

# The Last Time Around

**W**hile I was thrilled to return for a 25th and final season at Purdue, our non-conference schedule was brutal in 2004-05, and we could not recover from a 1-5 start. Our schedule was rated the most difficult among Division I schools, and I would have to agree. The only other time we had the nation's most difficult schedule was during my second season at Purdue in 1981-82, when we had a stretch of six consecutive defeats, including losses to DePaul, Louisville, Kentucky, and Syracuse.

We opened my final season with an 81-71 loss at Miami (Ohio), which should have received a 2005 NCAA tournament bid ahead of Northern Iowa. That was the first of 21 defeats to go with only seven victories. My philosophy always has been that when I have a young team, I should assemble an easier non-conference schedule and play most of our games at home. If I have an older team, it is good to go on the road and play a more difficult schedule, so that a veteran team is not overconfident.

However, during my final few seasons, we received a lot of complaints from fans about our home schedule. So we signed contracts with some teams in 2004-05 who we were not able to defeat. We played Oklahoma and Memphis during a five-day stretch in early December in Mackey Arena, losing by a combined 29 points. Cincinnati and North Carolina State also were on our schedule before Christmas, so we really never gave ourselves a chance to compete against some of the nation's elite with what was a relatively inexperienced team.

My final team also was plagued by injuries. Guard David Teague, who was our leading returning scorer, suffered a broken hand during preseason workouts and really struggled to shoot the basketball during November and December. Forward Matt Kiefer injured a knee in December and missed a couple of games. Point guard Bryant Dillon and our best player, forward Carl Landry, were both lost to knee injuries during Big Ten season. It was one thing after another. The injury to Landry was the final blow.

But people do not want to hear excuses, and I don't want to give excuses. We shot only 42.1 percent from the field and were 1-12 in games played away from Mackey Arena. Those numbers have losing season written all over them. I have no regrets whatsoever from that final season, other than my wife was unhappy about the ending. That bothers me, but all I know is that I tried my best. The sad thing is that while I was receiving gifts and tributes everywhere we went, our kids were

**My wife, Pat, and I appreciated all of the heartfelt thanks we received from Purdue fans, my players, the university, and opposing teams and coaches throughout the 2004-05 season.** *Purdue Sports Information*

not being rewarded for their hard work. I wanted the season to be about them and not about me. However, it certainly was nice that everyone seemed to appreciate what we accomplished at Purdue during 25 wonderful seasons.

I think the thing I appreciated most was that our fans stayed to honor me after we lost to Minnesota (59-57) on February 26, 2005 in my final game in Mackey Arena. We lost a heartbreaker, and the fans had a right to leave after the game. But no one left. That was very special to Pat and me. I just wish we could have done better for everyone during our final season. I had been thinking about what that final game would be like for five or six years and had decided that I wanted to leave on a winning note like boxer Rocky Marciano. I guess I picked my poison the wrong way.

All of the tributes to me were special. I am sorry that I did not get to experience what Ohio State had planned for me on February 2—a game that we lost 75-65—but I was sick with the flu, which is the only time in 47 years of coaching that I was unable to attend a game. The gifts I received were overwhelming. There's plenty of golf to be played: Wisconsin arranged for a golf outing at Whistling Straits; Michigan State set up a trip to Bay Harbour; and Ohio State sent me to a wonderful course, too. As a group, the Big Ten coaches sent Pat and me to Pebble Beach in California. Bruce Weber and Illinois gave me a grill, two new suits, a cell phone for two years, and a trip to two golf courses in the Chicago area. Iowa's gift was a trip to the Rio in Las Vegas, along with golf privileges at two of that city's finest golf courses. Purdue gave Pat and me a trip to Scotland and a cruise. I guess when people want to get rid of someone, they shower them with nice gifts.

I coached my final Purdue game on March 10, 2005, in the Big Ten Tournament in Chicago's United Center, where Iowa defeated us 71-52. The irony is that my final Purdue victory—a three-point win on February 16, 2005—also was registered against Iowa. Now, that it's over at Purdue, I realize that we had a heck of a ride. I wish we could have gone to the Final Four at least once. We got close several times, but it was not to be. If going to the Final Four or winning a Final Four was a priority for me, I probably should have changed jobs.

However, I don't think I am done coaching yet. I think something is going to come up. But my time at Purdue is over.

✦ ✦ ✦ ✦

As I experienced my final season, I thought about the many assistants who had helped me during our 25-year ride. Obviously, Bruce Weber—with all the success he has had in a short time at Illinois—was extremely special to me. He was a guy who was a diamond in the rough. I think we all took Bruce for granted. It's amazing that during my final seasons, fans said the reason we began to lose is because Bruce Weber left the program, first for Southern Illinois and now for Illinois. I joked with people, "Wait a minute, this is the guy I wanted to fire for about three seasons."

Frank Kendrick also was special, because Frank could really relate to kids, which was key when recruiting them. Jay Price, who is now on Bruce's staff at Illinois, was a hard worker for me and a real detail guy. Jay is very intelligent. Even though Tracy Webster worked only one year for us before going to Illinois with Bruce, I really liked Tracy, too.

The best thing about my 25th and final season was my staff: associate head coach and now head coach Matt Painter, and assistants Cuonzo Martin, Todd Foster, and Paul Lusk. They worked hard, planned well, and scouted efficiently. One of the problems our final staff may have had is that all of them were good college players. In turn, those guys, who were self-disciplined, have trouble with modern-day kids, because this generation of player is not as dedicated as guys like Matt, Cuonzo, and Todd. Todd has trouble with guys who are not tough. Cuonzo has trouble with guys who are not committed. Matt has trouble with guys who are not smart. That has been a difficult adjustment for them, but they will be okay.

I think it is important those coaches look ahead and not dwell on what took place during my final season. I read a book by New York Yankees manager Joe Torre in which he writes about playing with the great Hank Aaron, who told Torre that every at-bat marks the beginning of a new day. That is how Aaron chose to focus on a situation. I've tried to take that approach with my golf game, and I hope Matt Painter and his staff will take that approach as they rebuild Purdue basketball.

✦ ✦ ✦ ✦

For me, I will continue to enjoy the things that I love. Most people know that I am a big baseball fan. I love the game's strategy, and I enjoy watching baseball on television, I like the White Sox, Cubs, and Braves, but I'm a true Yankee fan who always watches them when they are on TV.

Of course, my friends know that it's easy to find me when the weather is nice, because I'm always on a golf course. I experienced one of the great thrills of my life in the spring of 2005, when I had the opportunity to play Augusta National. It's difficult to secure an invitation to play there. Talk about two days of highlights—everything we did was a highlight. And I almost made a hole in one on the par-3 16th hole. That was a gift from Kevin Stallings, who played for me and now is the head coach at Vanderbilt University.

Having the opportunity to play Augusta National was a tremendous experience, just as it was a tremendous experience to be the head coach of the Purdue basketball team for 25 seasons. Now that I am away from the day-to-day operations of the Purdue basketball program, I really don't miss it. After 47 years in the coaching business, I've seen it all and enjoyed it all. I'm not sure how I could top it. Purdue was the best place for me. I was interested in a strong academic school like Purdue, and since I grew up in an agriculture community, being at a university that stressed agriculture was important to me. Of course, Indiana is a basketball state, and that was very important to me as well.

We never won a national championship, but we had countless rewarding moments, both on and off the basketball court. Had you told me when I was 15 that I would eventually have the opportunity to experience and achieve what I have as a college basketball coach, I would have told you that you were nuts.